MW00695497

This is no longer
property of
King County Library System

My Renaissance

BELLEVUE REGIONAL LIBRARY
1111 116th NE
BELLEVUE, WA 98004

A Capital Discoveries Book

A series that features journeys of self-discovery, transformation,
inner-awareness, and recovery.

Other Capital Discoveries Books

Reading Water: Lessons from the River
REBECCA LAWTON

A lyrical journey down some of America's greatest rivers by one of the first female
river guides in the west.

There's a Porcupine in My Outhouse:
Misadventures of a Mountain Man Wannabe
MICHAEL J. TOUGIAS

A lively, often hilarious tale about a naïve flatlander's transformation into a dedicated mountain man—written by a well-known outdoor writer and syndicated
columnist.

Rivers of a Wounded Heart: Every Man's Journey
MICHAEL WILBUR

Combining contemporary psychotherapy and Native American wisdom, this
provocative memoir will sweep through the rivers of your own soul.

Touching Quiet: Reflections in Solitude
MINDY WEISEL

A celebrated artist's journey—how solitude inspired her work and calmed her soul.
Beautiful full-color paintings featured in each chapter.

Ancient Wisdom: A Chinese Calligrapher's Tale
P. ZBAR

"Chinese calligraphy, philosophy, and wisdom brought to brilliant life for a western
audience." —*Midwestern Book Review*

My Renaissance

A Widow's Healing
Pilgrimage to Tuscany

Rose Marie Curteman

CAPITAL
BOOKS, INC.

STERLING, VIRGINIA

Copyright © 2002 by Rose Marie Curteman

All rights reserved. No part of this book may be reproduced or utilized in any form or by any means, electronic or mechanical, including photocopying, recording, or by any information storage and retrieval system, without permission in writing from the publisher. Inquiries should be addressed to:

Capital Books, Inc.
P.O. Box 605
Herndon, Virginia 20172-0605

Library of Congress Cataloging-in-Publication Data

Curteman, Rose Marie.
  My renaissance : a widow's healing pilgrimage to Tuscany / Rose Marie
  Curteman.—1st ed. p. cm
  ISBN 1-892123-91-6 (alk. paper)
  1. Curteman, Rose Marie. 2. Widows—United States—Bibliography. 3. Renan,
  John—Death and burial. 4. Alzheimer's disease—Patients—Family
  relationships. 5. Bereavement. 6. Widows—Travel—Italy—Tuscany. I. Title.

HQ1058.5.US C87 2002
305.48'9654'092—dc21
  [B]   2002022408

Printed in Canada on acid-free paper that meets the American National Standards Institute Z39-48 Standard.

First Edition

10 9 8 7 6 5 4 3 2 1

Author's Note: To protect the privacy of others, I have changed all names and some indentifying facts.

This book is dedicated to

my sister Carole

for her brave and gallant spirit.

$\mathcal{M}$y own recovery, I realize, was greatly furthered by the love, understanding, and support of those around me. But I was also indebted to many unknown friends who had gone before me and left their testimony to illumine the shadowy path. In return I leave my own record, bearing witness to my journey, for others who may follow.

"It is, after all," as another writer has stated, "the only treasure, the only heirloom we have to leave—our own little grain of truth." Truth that is locked up in the heart—or in a diary—is sterile. It must be given back to life so that "the hour of lead"—of others—may be transmuted.

—Anne Morrow Lindbergh,
Hour of Gold, Hour of Lead,
on the death of her child.

Contents

Acknowedgments

*B*oundless thanks to my agent, Ed Knappman, of New England Publishing Associates, for his vision. I think of him as a true wise man who helped me understand that what we really need in our lives is not more tales of losses, but testimonies on how to heal from the losses that beset us. I can't imagine that this book would exist if it were not for psychologist Patricia Weenolsen, Ph.D., and freelance editor Phyllis Hatfield. I think of them both as angels. Judy Karpinski of Capital Books, Inc., has been a guiding light as have been the following individuals with whom I've been privileged to travel on this book-writing path: Sue Bender, Laura Connor, Dr. and Mrs. Hugh Dickinson, Dawn Dufford, Wick Dufford, Rosalie Gillman, Georgia Green, Lawrence Hamblen, Professor Emeritus Norris G. Haring, Sarah Jobs, Ph.D., George B. McDonald, M.D., Sally and Harry Prior, Christine Clifton-Thornton, Anthony P. Via, S.J., Ph.D., and Don Wright. And finally, loving thanks to my family, who affirm for me each day that the world is a good place: Mother, Carole, Franco, Mercedes, Fabrizio, Anne Katherine, Nicola, Antonio, Alexia, Alexandra, Alessandro, Taddeo, Clara, Ursel, Hans-Jörg, Bernd, Ariane, Daniela, Helmut, and Vicky.

Introduction

"I admit I seek balm for my disenchantment."
—ROBERT DESSAIX, *Night Letters*

This is the story of my midlife romance and marriage to my beloved husband, John, his long dying from Alzheimer's disease, and my healing journey to Tuscany.

Many others with losses such as mine have written moving accounts of their ordeals, and many professionals have given helpful advice about how to recover. Throughout John's journey into darkness, I was heartened by the experiences of those, like Anne Morrow Lindbergh, who had gone before me and "left their testimony to illumine the shadowy path." Their truths and resolve brought me more lasting solace than any quick-fix, self-help manuals. Sometimes we need to access the deeply personal inner feelings of others that reflect our own longings and quest for resolution. I found some memoirs that spoke to these concerns, but not enough. I hope that my own memoir will help others connect not only with my loss and grief, but more important, with my healing process, my personal renaissance.

John and I fell in love and married when I was in my late forties and he was in his early seventies. Many people reminded us of our age difference, often inadvertently and in amusing ways. We knew we didn't have much time together, but we intended to live fully and love completely during whatever years were left to us. As it happened, we had only one. Our coming apart took five grinding years during which I cared for him. In the end, as Alzheimer's stole his mind, he knew me only fleetingly. On one level the John I had married had become a body that must be bathed, a mouth into which food must be spooned, hips that must be cushioned, while I denied my own exhaustion day after day. On another level John was still who he was—his permanent Self, his beautiful soul. And it was this John with whom I connected. Thus, our love for one another persisted throughout our ordeal.

When John died, my loss felt deep and wide; a gaping darkness yawned at the center of my being. I knew that I would never get over it, that my loss would be with me always. But precisely how was I to cope? How could I knit myself back together so that I could live, and so that living would be worthwhile and meaningful again?

I am still here, I thought, *but what do I do with my hereness?*

I asked for help and waited for some prompting, but none came.

Fear and panic set in.

Is my life now a directionless life?

Then one day, I heard distant murmurs about *balm in beauty.*

Earlier in my life, before John's long dying, beauty had always comforted me—the turn of a marble column, the beauty of a redwinged blackbird, Albrecht Dürer's woodcuts, and the startling beauty of people from other cultures. But it had been so long since I had seen or felt or heard the beauty in anything, I thought the person I once had been had vanished forever.

Balm in beauty. I had read that beauty helps the soul grow wings. Now this thought galvanized me. *Maybe the sight of beauty can help bring balance to the horror of watching John die. Maybe it can help me fly again?*

Was it possible?

Slowly, the long-sought glimpse of healing possibilities appeared, distant at first, a hint of sunrise.

Before John became ill, I worked for a consortium of universities, one of which had a campus in Florence, Italy, where I had visited thirty-one years before and fallen in love with something beyond myself, and where later John and I spent days of joy. I decided to return to Florence as a midlife student in art history. I would be thirty to thirty-five years older than my fellow students, but my marriage had accustomed me to vast age discrepancies.

And so I went.

And I learned to live again.

PART I

LOVE

CHAPTER 1

The Spring of New Love

"[Love is] our highest word, and the synonym for God."
—RALPH WALDO EMERSON, *Essays*

John and I met at a fundraiser to benefit a college of the performing and visual arts. The room glistened with student art—murals, collages, and sculpture. Music majors tantalized us with Gershwin. Caterers served us champagne and crudités with seasoned salt on wicker trays. And the college's trustees and donor prospects mingled easily, relaxed by the effect of sparkling dry wine. A friend suggested that I meet an elegant-looking man hovering on the sidelines, basking in the festivities, yet holding himself above the fray.

"This is John Renan," a voice said as I reached out to shake the hand of a man who was nothing short of gorgeous.

I had heard of John. He was a trustee of the college, which had recently hired me to help raise money for educating professional artists. As such, he was one of my bosses. I had been told that he was "older"—late sixties—an accountant, divorced, successful—a nice human being. It was my business to meet him and involve him, as appropriate, in the school's fundraising objectives. It was not my business to get totally flustered the minute I laid eyes on him.

No one had told me that he was handsome—tall (taller than I, and in heels I stand six feet), with warm brown eyes, silver hair, and a lean physique. Creases around his eyes told me that he laughed a lot.

"Could I get you a drink?" he said casually after we shook hands.

Mildly flustered by his sheer good looks, I replied, "Ah . . . yes, water, please." I realized with a flush that in an artistic crowd, mine was hardly a chic response. If my composure had been better, I could at least have said, "Perrier," but I wasn't fast enough on my feet.

John brought me the water, said a few words, and was soon engaged in another conversation with someone else.

Some considered John a catch. Knowing that he had been single for over a dozen years, I thought, *There's probably something wrong with him once you get to know him. Considering the shortage of eligible men in his age bracket, if he were really okay, he wouldn't have lasted this long.* But these rationalizations betrayed my feelings. He had affected me at a deep level.

After our initial encounter I ran into John at occasional social gatherings to which he often arrived with a stately matron in tow. He and I were acquaintances, but we moved in different circles: he in the world of business, tennis, bridge, and cruises; I in the world of fund development, cooking, gardening, and occasional travel. I continued to admire him, but put any serious thoughts out of my mind. Yet my subliminal attraction would not go away. In fact, when I saw him with these older women—women who could be my mother—I felt a twinge of jealousy. And yet, they were John's age. I was not.

While John was somewhat of an icon, he was also approachable.

Impulsively one day, about a year after I met him, I invited him to attend a lecture on cancer research by a physician with whom I knew he sometimes played tennis.

After the cancer research evening, he reciprocated almost immediately. *Courtesy*, I told myself at first.

But he invited me out again and again and again.

*J*ohn knew everything. He had read every book ever written. He danced. He hiked. He played championship tennis and golf. He spoke Spanish and was studying German. He could recite poetry. He had wonderful eyes and hands like a pianist. He was quiet, but when he spoke, his intentions thundered. And he could laugh until tears streamed down his face.

After we had been dating for a while, I learned I could count on John. Once when I was in a late-night car accident and had to be taken to an emergency room, he rushed to my side saying, "We're in this together." He didn't leave me until I was back on my feet.

When shingles fell off my roof or pipes leaked, he repaired them (or tried to). After I invited him to dinner, he couldn't wait to wash the dishes, reminding me often that he was "fully domesticated."

He brought me Christmas trees and poinsettias. He took me on picnics and ferry rides. He toured me through the Olympic National Forest and the lower elevations of Mount Rainier. He took me to operas and symphonies. He introduced me to regional wineries. He taught me to tango.

To know him was to feast on life.

John knew that I had taught English literature right after graduating from college. With some pride, he quoted from Thomas Gray's

"Elegy Written in a Country Churchyard." He could recite portions of William Wordsworth's "Ode: Intimations of Immortality": *Our birth is but a sleep and a forgetting; / The Soul that rises with us, our life's Star; / Hath had elsewhere its setting, / And cometh from afar: / Not in entire forgetfulness, / And not in utter nakedness, / But trailing clouds of glory do we come . . .*

Later, as John's world diminished, I wondered if his interest in those lines might have come from his unconscious need to be reassured of our immortality.

A high point during our courtship years occurred when he announced to me one day, "My goal in life is to have you love me as much as you loved Champ," my late collie dog. Although he said it in jest, deep down I knew that he meant it.

By 1987, three years had passed since John and I met. Three years of warm and loving friendship, but the subject of marriage had never come up in any formal way. And I didn't press for anything more. *After all, I rationalized, this man is seventy. I'm forty-six. How much time would I have with someone his age? Five years? Ten years? Relationships don't always have to be formalized,* I continued to reason. *They can just be enriching, here-and-now encounters that expose us to interests and ideas that might otherwise never come our way.*

But then something changed.

I told John that I would be flying off to see my family, who live in Germany, but were then on a three-week tour exploring the American West.

"I'm going to meet my mother and stepfather for a few days," I announced casually.

John met this news with complete silence—at least for a moment. Then in a voice that sounded almost adolescent, he replied, "I want to go too."

His interest in going surprised me; he had been so nonchalant about making a serious commitment to our relationship.

"Why do you want to go?" I asked, taken aback by a response that struck me as pushy.

"In case we get married, I want to have met them," he said matter-of-factly, as if he had been thinking about it but hadn't gotten around to discussing it with me.

I was thunderstruck. He had finally said the "M" word. From that point forward, we began openly to explore the possibility of marriage.

Sometime later, with the subject of marriage firmly on the table, I asked John, "What took you so long?"

He replied, "I was afraid you'd say no." He went on to say that he didn't dare believe that I would be interested in someone his age. Much later, as we reflected on our life together, I asked him about our first date and why he had plunged into our relationship with such zeal.

"I was waiting for you," he answered.

My family liked John and were not put off by the age difference. During private moments when John discreetly excused himself so that I could visit with them alone, my mother reminded me about an old European view: "Women mature faster than men," she said encouragingly, "and if you marry an older man, his psychological maturity will have had time to catch up with yours."

She must have seen how eager I was to hear more. She continued: "Love later in life is different from when you're young. How we look isn't as important as what we become—our quality of being—our integrity, humanity, decency—that's what attracts an older lover. Physical limitations later in life matter less than spiritual ones."

It was all music to my ears.

*P*ractical considerations tempered our haste to formalize our bond—the main being the "high risk" nature of what marriage counselors call an "age-discrepant marriage." He was twenty-four years my senior!

My personal experience with older men had been that they die young. My grandfather died at 72, an uncle at 73, and still another uncle at 74. That scared me. Yet I knew there were also those remarkable long-lived people like Pablo Casals, Arthur Rubinstein, George Bernard Shaw, and Michelangelo. Not everyone died young.

While John and I weighed the pros and cons of an age discrepancy as vast as ours, we also asked ourselves if it wasn't finally time to live life on our own terms? John no longer suffered the agony of needing other people's approval, and I liked that. When I suggested that he consider replacing his twelve-year-old Buick, he grumbled, "Why? I have no one I want to impress."

To explore further our concerns about our age disparity, I asked John to go with me to a clinical psychologist, a specialist in age.

Dr. Jackman, a man in his mid-sixties, rhapsodized that age is just not what it used to be. "Sixty-five today is more like fifty was a couple of generations ago. Chronological age alone no longer necessarily determines how we behave and live. Those who study aging now think more in terms of biological age, which gauges how well the body works, not how long it's been around." He went on to say that eighty-five now marks the advent of old age and that in the not too distant future we would see old age setting in around ninety to one hundred.

We were buoyed by our discussion with Dr. Jackman. In a sense, he had given us permission to get married. "Good luck," he said as he showed us to the door.

I had every reason to believe his encouraging portrayal of age applied to John. I wanted John to be one of those lucky seniors with the right genetic inheritance and mindset to flourish in his later years. And I convinced myself that he would. From all I could tell, John easily passed the test of successful biological aging. After all, he never smoked. He rarely drank. He exercised. His father lived into his nineties, his mother into her eighties. John was in for some good years, I felt sure.

Still, after meeting with Dr. Jackman, I went to the public library to read further about "May-December marriages." I learned that they have long been socially acceptable. In fact, historically, these marriages were the most desirable marital arrangement. The only question has been in deciding the optimum age difference between the partners. The French suggest a prospective female partner's age should be based on the man's: half his age plus seven is their equation for marital bliss. This seems appropriate to current standards for a male who is in his twenties; a man of twenty-eight, for instance, would marry a woman of twenty-one. However, the difference increases with age: a man of seventy-eight, by the same calculation, would marry a woman of forty-six—a thirty-two-year difference. The Greek philosopher Aristotle does away with arithmetic altogether, suggesting that a man should choose a wife of half his years—with the stipulation that he not marry until the age of thirty-six.

Although a wider difference in ages between spouses may have been common in the past, today America's young often find fault with the old, who do, indeed, sometimes sell themselves short. But there are legions, my reading emphasized, who only in their later years come to full flowering.

John, I wanted to believe, was one of them.

Those who belong to these illustrious legions were portrayed as knowing so much, as having a grace, a charm, a vigor, a productiveness, and even a passion that they might not have had earlier in life. They understand that life is short, and because it is, they appreciate its gifts and beauties. They live more in the moment. They postpone fewer things. They are no longer slaves to conformity. They are freer. They are more considerate of others. They have explored what really matters and have concluded that, in a relationship, it is love that really matters, not sexual prowess.

But the authorities noted that older men, no matter how enlightened, can bring their own variety of problems into a relationship. They can be set in their ways. They can be rigid and inflexible if they had earlier tendencies in that direction. They probably have been married before, as John and I had been. Like John, they may have adult children who might take offense if their father decides to remarry—a major barrier to a successful marriage. The older man might have sexual needs and expectations different from those of his new partner. An older man might satisfy his much younger wife at first, but sexual fulfillment of the early passionate days of any relationship can quickly wane.

And then there is the matter of facing illness and death. We will all die, I was reminded again and again, and illness, often long and drawn out, is the most likely avenue to death's door.

I believed all the good things and denied all the bad. I wanted to marry John. I was crazy about him and I was still buoyant from our talk with Dr. Jackman, who had reinforced what I already felt.

 $\mathcal{M}$y biological parents divorced when I was eleven months old. Because by then, war in Germany was in full swing, my father was shipped off to battle and my mother to France as a secretary for the armed forces. I went to live with my maternal grandparents, Opa, sixty-two, and Oma, fifty-two, who raised me until I was eight. My experience with them was one of unconditional love. It has been the purest commitment I have known. It gave me a lifelong sense of self-acceptance. I remember feeling puzzled when I first experienced rejection as a child in school. *How can they not like me?*

Before I came to them, my grandparents had grown apart. But soon after my arrival, they found themselves so happily absorbed in nurturing me that they became a united couple once again. For years thereafter, Oma told me, *"Du bist ein Geschenk vom lieben Gott"* (You are a gift from God).

It's lovely to grow up so valued.

Now I suspected that by marrying John, unconsciously I might have been trying to recreate the love and commitment I knew with Opa.

 $\mathcal{J}$ohn and I dismissed the so-called perils of chronological age as antiquated notions. To us, age was about fulfillment and accomplishment and marriage was a route to happiness.

We signed a prenuptial agreement. Although counseled by a lawyer as part of the prenuptial planning, he did not advise me to insist that John sign a living will—an advance directive stating his personal conditions about dying. John's own attorney later told me, "John is the only client I've ever had who has refused to sign a living will."

My oversight in not insisting on a living will would later prey on my mind. But at the time of our marriage, I wasn't thinking about illness or death. I thought only about life and immortality.

John and I married at my home on a golden May afternoon. The garden was a profusion of rhododendrons. I wore a lavender dress that I had sewn myself. John wore a gray suit with a necktie that I had given him. His eyes twinkled as he smiled shyly. To me, that day, he was more handsome than ever. A dozen family members and friends attended us. As the sun filtered through the cedars and hemlocks, we celebrated with champagne and cold salmon.

CHAPTER 2

Ti Amo Più Che Mai

("I love you more than ever.")

> "Marriage is by nature miraculous and magical. We do not
> understand it and cannot know where it is headed."
> —THOMAS MOORE, *Soul Mates*

After the wedding, we settled into John's old house in a section of Seattle called Madison Park, nestled pristinely on Lake Washington and in full view of the snow-capped Cascades just beyond.

"Just ten minutes from downtown," John liked to gloat when anyone even remotely challenged his decision to stay there while many of his contemporaries were moving into downtown condos.

His colonial-style house was John's piece of earth. He built it in the late 1940s. His father put the roof on it. He raised his children in it. When marriage was a serious possibility, he had asked me to understand his need to go on living there. It nurtured him. It was a source of peace.

Yet to my eyes, the place seemed a little timeworn—genteel neglect is the polite term. The yard had gone so long without adequate pruning that just walking from the public sidewalk to the front door was a test of courage. Once you opened the door, you were hit with a mauve-walled living room adorned with his former wife's artistic memorabilia. The kitchen could best be imagined by what I heard a relative propose to him one day: "Burn it down and start over."

Into this environment I married, albeit with promises of better things to come. And it was here that I met the notorious Sally, John's cleaning woman of many years.

"Please don't do anything to upset Sally," John pleaded with me when all I had done up to that point was say hello. Sally reigned over the house like a czarina. Wanting to ease into my new living arrangement with some grace, I encouraged Sally to continue her routine, until one day I discovered that she took John's vacuum cleaner to her other jobs. John's cleaning supplies went, too.

"Don't her other clients provide their own vacuum cleaners and cleaning supplies?" I asked John.

Somewhat embarrassed, he replied that he was aware of the situation but she always returned the machine and it was just not a big deal. While this matter was still up in the air, I also noted that Sally routinely washed out the inside of the refrigerator with the same water she had used to mop the kitchen floor. I didn't need to be microbiologist to know this practice was seriously unhygienic.

It grew apparent that Sally and I needed to compare notes—first on hygiene and then, quite simply, on borrowing other people's belongings. She acted the good sport, but eventually she left us to work in an office.

As for our Madison Park rain forest, we hired professional tree

cutters, pruners, and landscape architects. Whole armies descended on us with pruning sheers, tree loppers, blocks and tackles,
stump grinders, chainsaws, and boom machines. Like a good land
steward, John supervised the rout as best he could, arriving at work
late and leaving work early to ensure that those he had set loose on
his property would not take what he considered to be "unautho-
rized liberties."

But the war was on. D-Day in Madison Park. Occasionally, I
would find John negotiating for the survival of a particular branch,
other times grieving its demise.

"No, I don't want that cedar pruned on the right side," John
protested.

"But, Mr. Renan," the tree pruner said, "You'll have more sunlight
if you just take down those lower branches," and he pointed to a tree
that resembled something from a tropical jungle. "Besides, in a wind-
storm the tree could collapse. It could fall on your house."

Now John had second thoughts. Reluctantly and ever the conser-
vationist, he said, "Okay, then, but be sure you cut the branches for
firewood."

Once the buzzing sounds ended, our neighbors confided their
relief at the return of the sounds of silence and their view of Lake
Washington. Wrenched by the yard restoration, John later confessed: "The yard has never looked better." Indeed, once these
armies had completed their operations, we possessed a sanctuary
profuse with sunlight, flowers, squirrels, robins, and even pugnacious
raccoons.

The interior of the house changed, too. We didn't burn down the
kitchen as that relative had suggested; we just replaced it.

It took weeks of guttings, power shutdowns, water turnoffs, camping out on the dining room floor by candlelight with intermittent
suppers cooked on the rain-soaked barbecue outside, and weeks of

washing dishes by flashlight in the basement utility sink. It was a party! Occasional bottles of champagne obviously helped. Within six months our house became a charming home and a perfect backdrop for our life together.

As an afterthought to the remodeling project, we had the architect design separate but adjoining bedrooms on the second floor. John snored and it seemed that the more he settled into marriage, the more his nighttime cacophonies intensified. At times, to my exhausted ears, he might as well have roared from the rooftops. While the room shook, I lay awake trying to figure out what to do.

I thought of ear plugs. I thought of doctors—*there must be cures for snoring disorders*. From my days as an English teacher, I remembered Lady Macbeth referring to sleep as the "season of all nature," and I wasn't getting enough of this essential ingredient. In desperation, I took disgruntled trips across the hall to where John's exclamations couldn't reach my ears. Finally, I knew the only solution: separate, but adjoining bedrooms that allowed lots of visiting back and forth.

We could have moved into a hotel during the remodeling, but John would have missed the chaos—the charge, the fire that comes from pandemonium. This was life! John liked taking the ragged edges of a jigsaw puzzle and weaving them together. As for me, I was usually ready for a good adventure, and this was hardly boredom.

At seventy-two John's energy soared. Nothing was tedious or hard for him. "I never get tired," he'd say. Usually I'd be looking for the nearest couch long before John was ready to quit.

Soon he proclaimed, "My tennis game is improving," the ultimate test of his well-being.

John had long been a tennis buff, delighting in the game's energy and thrust—the powerful serve, the sure-fire volley, the point determined. And then the probe for weakness, the offense, the defense—these had taken on a whole new edge. It was as though the neurotransmitters of joy had permeated every facet of his life.

Our weekend routine: Friday night we played tennis with friends. Saturday morning, during the football season, we hosted a pre-game brunch in our home. In the early afternoon we attended a college football game. We'd spend the evening at a dance. Sunday, we'd take in a professional football game. Sunday night, we were off to the theater. Monday would find me crawling back to work just to get some rest. If John was an old man, it was news to me.

After our marriage, John shortened his office hours and plunged into domesticity. He treated simple tasks of homemaking with a kind of reverence. Bed making, for example: Once he was fully relocated in his own bedroom, he deemed that only he could adequately make his bed. Each morning, like a military tactician, he began the meticulous alignment of sheets—stretching, pulling, turning, yanking, right-angled curves, perfect tucks. Silver quarters could bounce off his covers.

As for the laundry, only an advanced degree in physics could prepare you for doing the wash in our house—sorting of colors (lights, darks, mediums)—weights, textures, and proportions—the deliberations on brands of detergents—the decision to use or not use bleach—then the meticulous adjustment of cycles (energy saving, water saving, permanent press, regular heat). Major stuff. Then the folding of the laundry—again with military precision on a counter designed just for that purpose. Eventually, the thoughtful trips to the linen closet where sheets and towels were organized into something like a lending library—the Dewey Decimal System of Linen Closets: "your stuff," "my stuff," small items, medium, and large, color coding. Suffice it to say, the system worked.

These tasks—bed making, the laundry, and others—were more than household tasks. They were meditations, acts of love. With age, I began to realize, life takes on a whole new cast. It becomes more beautiful, more poignant. Just to watch the morning light amble across the back deck, to see the rain caress the ivy, to hear a child's laughter, or simply to make the bed or do the laundry—these become sacred acts. Moments that in youth John might have squandered carelessly, he now harbored like gold.

"What does this new life mean to you—the marriage, the new responsibilities?" I asked John one evening after dinner as we sat in the family room reflecting on our lives.

"Something to live for," he replied easily.

On the anniversary of our first six months of marriage—November 1988—John arrived home from work with an armload of fresh flowers, announcing, "Happy six-months anniversary!" He then handed me a small box. On velvet lay a gold charm inscribed in Italian: *Ti Amo Più Che Mai.* I awaited him with a tassel of balloons and a bottle of champagne.

We were off to a good start.

PART II

LOSS

CHAPTER 3

In A Gloomy Wood

"Marriage is not a love affair, it's an ordeal. It is a religious exercise, a sacrament, the grace of participating in another life."
—JOSEPH CAMPBELL,
A Joseph Campbell Companion

Almost from the beginning of our marriage, John lost weight. In fact, he had lost a few pounds just before our wedding, but he liked that.

"I'm trimming down," he told me proudly. "Getting in shape."

But the weight continued to drop, even with increased caloric intake.

Complete checkups came back negative. "Side effects of the normal aging process," was the standard medical explanation. Still his weight fell. One pound here, two pounds there, until his scale dipped from the 190s into the 160s—and this for a man well over six feet tall. I began to worry. If John worried, he didn't let on. He just laughed it off with a playful, "Wouldn't want a bay window."

New and unfamiliar naps before dinner, naps after dinner. A failing tennis serve. Stooped posture. His left arm strangely no longer swinging when he walked. A handwriting whose script became noticeably smaller. More doctors. Second opinions. Third opinions. All came back negative. We wondered about going to the Mayo Clinic. The considered medical answer was no: Mayo doesn't have any medical resources that Seattle doesn't have.

He began experiencing muscular rigidity. A shuffle. Trouble swallowing. An irregular heartbeat. Frequent medical exams showed no diagnosable problem.

I contacted a gastroenterologist friend, a former neighbor, hoping that he would tell me that John's symptoms were something else.

On talking with him, I emphasized the dramatic weight loss—thirty pounds in just months.

Not knowing any particulars other than my distraught portrayal of his symptoms, the gastroenterologist's first response was, "It's either an absorption problem or inadequate caloric intake."

"Yes, absorption," I cried hopefully, grabbing at anything that sounded halfway reasonable.

John can't assimilate his food, or maybe I just haven't been feeding him enough, I told myself, trusting that with just some minor adjustment his failing condition would reverse. In addition to his regular meals, I began giving him generous portions of a high-calorie, nutritionally balanced beverage.

His symptoms persisted for well over a year. Finally, after consulting more doctors and undergoing still more tests, we learned that John did not have an absorption problem.

"John has Parkinson's disease," a neurologist offered soberly. "It's a common but progressive disorder of the part of the brain that controls movement."

John and I glanced at each other with a look that said, "The doctor must be wrong. It's just clumsiness that comes with aging."

But we listened as the neurologist continued, "While there's no cure, we can treat it symptomatically and often effectively. I have some patients who are doing well ten and twenty years after diagnosis."

He handed John two pamphlets about the disease. "I suggest you read these. Come back in a couple of weeks and we'll discuss medications that can help relieve some of your symptoms."

We left the doctor's office shaken, but also hopeful that the diagnosis might be wrong. As we walked to the parking garage, confusion washed over me.

But we were just married! . . . our marriage was supposed to be a new lease on life . . . a new beginning . . . touched by grace . . . impervious to misfortune . . . but now . . .

Parkinson's disease, we learned from our reading, is a disorder of the small part of the brain called the substantia nigra. Nerve cells in the substantia nigra have a way of undergoing a little-understood and rapid death, depriving the brain of a chemical called dopamine, a neurotransmitter essential for normal human movement. As dopamine-producing cells in the substantia nigra die, symptoms of Parkinsons's disease arise—symptoms that had become familiar terrain to us: feeling slow and tired, stillness, shuffling, a stooped gait, a soft monotone voice, but strangely, in John's case, no involuntary trembling, which textbooks described as typical. No cure exists for this progressive brain disease, from which about one million Americans suffer, but drug therapy enables some patients to enjoy a relatively normal life for five to twenty years after diagnosis.

The word "progressive" gave us pause. The disease was still in the early stages. Things would get worse, maybe, but for now we had time to process the diagnosis and develop a battle plan.

After consulting yet another doctor who ordered yet more tests, we had to accept that John had Parkinson's disease, plain and simple. He had entered the uncharted territory of illness, and I, by force of circumstance, had entered it right along with him.

On the positive side, as fearsome as any illness is, at least we had a label for the symptoms that had been stalking John. By defining the enemy we were better able to mobilize against it. We read more about Parkinson's disease. We talked with other patients and found that many were managing well. One friend told us, "I'm leading the good life in the slow lane."

We were optimistic.

John had never been seriously ill and had no great respect for the medical profession. "I don't like pills and I don't like doctors," he complained, as he began to realize that palliatives might well become a part of his life.

Always pushing hope, I offered, "But John, doctors have also given us wondrous technological breakthroughs. Where would we be without polio vaccine, pacemakers, bypass, and hip replacement surgeries?"

But it was too soon to approach him with logic. He was mired in frustration, even anger.

At the root of his ire, I sensed a profound fear of losing control. He hated the thought that some other force might assume supremacy over his life.

My own feelings about John's diagnosis were surprise and relief that it wasn't anything worse. *Parkinson's is so treatable,* I thought. We had heard so many success stories. Besides, I wanted to believe we were still on the fast track to happiness.

While John responded well to treatment, we were shadowed by the knowledge that this was a progressive disease. Over time his symptoms would worsen. Quietly and behind the scenes, I explored alternative forms of medicine, classical Chinese acupuncture among them. John, I knew, was conventional in his medical thinking. But I also knew that he had an open mind. He had traveled widely in China. He respected that culture. *Perhaps,* I thought, *he would be amenable to acupuncture as a complement to the conventional treatment he is receiving.* I outlined my scheme, but John hesitated. He stalled.

Months went by. But as he noticed a subtle worsening of his symp-toms—greater fatigue and more stiffness—he said, "Okay, I'll go just to listen to the acupuncturist."

John did submit to one trial session, but in the end he chose not to return. The experience was too outlandish for his more conven-tional belief system.

I groped for anything that would make John well again. Exercise. A rowing machine. A stationary bike. Walks. Fresh air. Vitamins. Minerals. Protein drinks. I even contacted a spiritual healer on the East Coast who, I was told, had helped someone in Seattle beat cancer.

"Do you make house calls?" I asked.

"I could possibly come out to Seattle in two months' time but unless the client were completely receptive, my efforts would be in vain." I thought of my practical husband and thanked the healer for his time.

In the end, we settled for conventional medical treatment.

John was a proud man. Illness embarrassed him. He tried to min-imize it, and he did a good job.

One Sunday afternoon, shortly after the diagnosis, I found him sitting pensively in his burgundy recliner. I had just finished baking a chocolate cake. John had a sweet tooth and if I didn't have some-thing delectable in the house at all times, I had failed him as a wife.

"What's for dessert?" he usually asked before inquiring about the main course.

I sat down beside him and asked softly, "What are you thinking?"

He looked up. I could tell he wanted to talk. He started to say something . . . then, never one to complain, he paused . . .

I kissed his forehead.

He took a deep breath.

After more prodding by me and still more hesitation by him, he finally said plaintively, "All this work . . . all these years of effort . . . and for what?"

My heart ached for him. I knew what he was getting at. His gloom was more than the diagnosis of Parkinson's. It was age and its inevitabilities—the gradual letting go of all he had cherished and toiled to attain.

John was by now in his early seventies. However benign a disorder appears at the outset, it is still the most likely course to life's unyielding end . . . *to give up all that I have struggled to attain . . . the omnipotence of death and its chilling proximity to our lives* . . . I sensed his thinking.

After World War II John had launched himself in business and had survived and even prospered while others failed. He had a broad circle of friends that reached back to high school. He had cultivated interests as varied as horticulture, tennis, and Hindu temples. And now, late in life, he had embarked on a new marriage.

To even think about giving all that up . . .

I wanted to help him—the question was how to do it in a way that would honor his plight and show that I had heard him fully.

I took his hand and said quietly, "But, John, you heard what the doctor said, Parkinson's is so treatable. Even ten and twenty years after diagnosis, patients are still doing well. And you heard what Dr. Jackman said about age these days—old age doesn't even set in until eighty-five. You've got a ways to go!" I added wanting to sound cheerful.

He looked up skeptically.

Then something from deep inside compelled me to say, "Whatever happens, John, I'll never leave you. You can count on me."

He put his arm around me, wrapped his other hand around mine and kissed it.

After another pause, I said, "It's Sunday . . . I've just baked a cake . . . Let's have a piece and then go for a walk."

He wasn't finished with his depression, but he did have a piece of cake and we did go for a walk.

*F*or some time John had sensed that something was wrong beyond Parkinson's disease. I was suspicious too, but he regularly saw two top-flight physicians, an internist and a neurologist, who assured us that his symptoms were simply "part of the normal aging process." I wanted to believe them. But the body that for decades had served John flawlessly had now begun to fail him. He was making serious mistakes. Spatial relationships had become a particular problem.

One night as John pulled his car into our garage, he smashed the right front fender into a cabinet in which we stored empty glass canning jars. (We occasionally canned pears from our now well-pruned-and-tended pear tree!)

The garage exploded with glass.

Frantic, John raced to the kitchen to find me.

"There's an emergency in the garage!" he cried in a state of agitation that I had never before seen in this usually tranquil man.

I ran to the garage where I found broken glass everywhere, the car engine still running, and a battered automatic garage door mechanism rotating recklessly.

By now experience had taught me to stay calm during John's failings. The calmer I was, the calmer he was.

"Don't worry," I said in a tone that I hoped would soothe his panic. "This is nothing to worry about. Why don't you come back into the kitchen with me now and have supper. We have pasta and ice cream. We can clean this up later."

John seemed relieved. He needed things to be okay and he liked to be directed. As soon as I turned off the car engine and switched off the garage door opener, he trudged back to the kitchen with me and we enjoyed a peaceful meal. He nearly forgot about the incident. After supper he followed me back to the garage for a quick look. Then his attention lapsed. Oblivious to the fact that we were standing in a sea of glass, he wanted to go to his study to open the day's mail.

About a year after the diagnosis of Parkinson's, I noticed that John, in addition to having problems with spatial relationships, seemed to be mildly disoriented. His ability to process information and solve problems faltered. In the past he had made our travel arrangements; now he passed these responsibilities to me. He hardly cared where we went. Flight schedules, seat assignments—details were increasingly irrelevant. In the past he had paid the household bills. Now bills languished unpaid on his desk until I paid them. John had always demonstrated a facility with words. Now I noticed a growing discrepancy between ideas he appeared to want to verbalize and what he actually said. He sometimes said, *"You* told me," when it was clear he meant, *"She* told me." He sometimes called his briefcase "the library," and the zipper in his trousers "my suspenders." He was increasingly exhausted for no apparent reason. He had trouble tying his shoelaces. Occasionally, he asked me to help him knot his tie.

Eighteen months after the diagnosis of Parkinson's, and three years after our marriage, John's neurologist was sufficiently concerned about these new symptoms that he ordered a whole new battery of tests—the usual medical history and physical, but with some different twists: a one-and-a-half day psychoneurological test, a CT scan, tests of mental function, and what seemed like memory games— "Name the presidents as far back as possible, starting with Bush."

Strange stuff. What are they looking for?

When the test results were in, the doctor called and said, "Rose Marie, I'd like to speak with you about John's condition alone. Could you come to my office tomorrow afternoon at 4:30?"

"You mean you don't want John to be present?" I asked, uncertain that I had understood him correctly.

"No, best not this time. The diagnosis is fairly serious and it could upset him."

When I came to his office the next afternoon, the grim-faced neurologist lost little time in telling me: "John has what is sometimes called a secondary sign of Parkinson's disease—dementia, a loss or impairment of mental powers." He then reported his stunning conclusion: "Alzheimer's disease is the most likely diagnosis."

Alzheimer's? John has Alzheimer's?

My head whirled in disbelief as I looked for some sign in the neurologist's face that would suggest doubt. But I saw nothing other than the expression of someone practiced in the art of conveying bad news. He was joyless and austere like his office—dark, heavy, unwelcoming.

Before I could grasp the implication of what the neurologist had said, he continued.

"There's no advantage in telling John. Even at this early stage of his illness, he would have only a short-lived understanding of what this diagnosis means. Talk to him about 'memory impairment.' There's no urgency, but you should begin to think about eventual systems for guardianship and care."

On that gray Seattle afternoon, I felt dazed as the doctor's words passed before me, as if through a glass, dim and shadowy.

Finally, I found my voice. "For some time, I've suspected that John had a problem beyond Parkinson's disease. But Alzheimer's—cerebral atrophy that will lead to death—never entered my mind."

For substantiation, the neurologist handed me a neatly typed, ten-page Confidential Neurological Evaluation, and pointed to page seven, saying, "You see, his progressive brain disease is already so advanced that his IQ has plummeted to 84."

I don't remember leaving his office or finding the elevator to the parking garage. I remember running into a friend who looked shocked at my appearance.

"Are you okay?" she asked.

"Yes." I answered, wanting to keep the diagnosis to myself, at least for the moment. *The doctor could be wrong,* I thought as I retreated from reality while adjusting to the crisis.

"Let's have dinner sometime," she called as she stepped into her car.

"Okay," I responded, as if John and I had a lifetime ahead of us.

*A*s the hours after the diagnosis passed and the reality of what I had just heard sank in, I felt as though the neurologist had pulled a pin on a grenade and thrown it at me. At the same time, I knew I couldn't wallow in self-pity.

I've got to notify John's sons, then schedule an appointment for John to meet with the neurologist.

And just when I needed more time, the consortium of universities for which I worked converted my job from part time to full time.

I felt under siege from all directions.

*W*hen John himself met with the neurologist, only cryptic messages were communicated.

"Memory impairment, that's what you've got, John," the neurologist intoned somewhat condescendingly.

He's written him off, I thought angrily.

I wanted the neurologist to explain further. I wanted to believe that John could still understand if he were just given the information in the right way—simply, in short words, in quiet tones.

John clung to every word, as if attentiveness alone might make things better. He probed the doctor's face for meaning. He wanted to hear, "We can make this affliction go away." But he only heard mumbo jumbo.

Disappointed, confused, and frustrated at the utter nonsensicality of it all, John suddenly erupted: "All these tests and nothing has been found!"

With measured words, the neurologist repeated what he had said before. The deceit had begun.

As we left the office, I had a moment alone with the neurologist. "Why didn't you tell John the truth?" I asked.

"John's condition has already progressed so far that he would have only a fleeting sense of what this diagnosis means. Besides, it's my experience that some patients who receive this kind of news might attempt suicide. Consider this a common preventive measure," the doctor said kindly but firmly.

After listening to the doctor's reasoning and reviewing again the contents of the psychoneurological report, I accepted his logic. It was clear that John no longer had the intellectual resources to process the complexities of brain biology. After witnessing his decline during the last few months and suspecting what the future would hold, I knew that for John, all that mattered now was maintaining a relative peace.

That evening as I lay in bed unable to sleep, I thought about an encounter with a stranger at the Honolulu Airport the previous year, on our return from a vacation in Maui.

As John and I made our way from one terminal to the next, I noticed that a fellow passenger, a pleasant-looking, middle-aged man, watched us with more than usual interest.

This was not uncommon. As a couple, we were an anomaly to some—at first glance we looked like father and daughter, not husband and wife. As we marched briskly through the airport corridors so as not to miss our connecting flight, the stranger kept pace, stealing discreet glances. When we reached our respective boarding areas and he was about to be directed to the left and we to the right, he approached me apologetically. "Excuse me. I couldn't help but notice you. Is the man you're with your husband or your father?"

"He's my husband," I laughed, knowing full well that we stood out in a crowd and that we had teased his imagination.

"The reason I asked," he offered sheepishly, "is that I'm currently thinking of marrying a woman who's thirty and I'm fifty-three. It's great right now, but what will it be like when she's fifty and I'm seventy-three?"

"It's wonderful," I answered, still drunk with the conceit of new love. "Do it. Marry her," I remember telling him flamboyantly. Even though we knew about Parkinson's at that point already, I still felt a glow around our lives.

Now, after hearing the diagnosis of Alzheimer's hours before, I wanted to retract everything I had said to that stranger that day in the Honolulu Airport so long ago.

"Don't do it! Don't even consider an age-discrepant marriage such as ours."

In the coming days a sea of emotions flooded through me.

Please, God, make this go away. We've got to beat this. I want to go back to the way things were. The promise of our marriage has turned to heartbreak. We've got to work with what is. I still believe in love and the ultimate good.

CHAPTER 4

An Abominable Region

"The purpose of a relationship is not to make you feel good
or even to make you happy. It's to help you grow and
to bring you closer to God."
—BARBARA DE ANGELIS, PH.D.,
For the Love of God

"Create as calm an environment as possible. Simplify his life. Reduce the number of messages you send to his damaged brain. Don't provoke him. Agree with everything. Let him save face." This from Dr. Demetrius, one of several doctors I had by then consulted for additional opinions.

I read everything I could get my hands on about the day-to-day management of demented patients. But what helped me more than anything else was my experience in the 1960s teaching high school students with cognitive disabilities who had IQs considerably lower than John's at this time.

Expect attention spans to be short.

Remember that their cognitive processes are slower; therefore, their response latency will lag.

Try to make clear what is going to happen next, so they can anticipate.

Don't forget that people with these disabilities benefit greatly from structure.

Allow them to experience some measure of success.

*A*fter diagnosis, John continued to go to his office as before. Work was a predictable destination, a safe routine. And I sensed it reassured John that he was still a person of the world.

Coworkers who had known him for decades kept an eye on his affairs; as the founder of his accounting firm, he would not be allowed to blunder.

"The last thing to be affected with an Alzheimer's patient is what he's always done," Dr. Demetrius told me. During these first months after diagnosis, John could still talk a good talk for ten minutes or so about the basic precepts of his work.

"Always remember that assets equal liabilities plus owner's equity. That's the most fundamental concept in accounting," I overheard him say to a friend one day.

I was impressed. And others who heard him paid attention, too, at least at first. But soon the same canned phrases came again. His repertoire had run dry. The mysterious disease that attacks and destroys brain cells had begun to pillage John's mind.

By now John no longer met with clients. He no longer oversaw financial matters. If a phone call came for him, the receptionist screened it. Soon phone calls stopped. People knew. Mainly John sat at his desk working on carefully selected projects. Sometimes, he only opened his mail.

He continued to lunch with old friends, who were saddened by his decline but became a caring circle. He attended football games. He worked in the yard, paying particular attention to his dahlia garden. In the spring, prior to his diagnosis, he had planted dahlia tubers in his usual fashion, burying them in a soil rich with organic matter, phosphorus, and potash. During the months after his diagnosis, he tended their growth, rejoicing over each until the once-frail dahlia stems were four and five feet tall, yielding ribbons of color that lasted until November.

On the down side, John's hand-eye coordination had slowed so much that he was forced to give up tennis. Increased muscular weakness made walking a chore. The most hurtful of all these early setbacks came when his internist and neurologist said, "John, you've got to give up driving."

John nearly cried. It broke his heart. It was an emasculation. It was entry into nonpersonhood. It was a herald of the end.

For months afterward, in his own burdened way, John fumed at the two doctors who had caused his driver's license and car insurance policy to be canceled. Alzheimer's is supposed to be about memory loss, but he remembered this indignity for a long time.

"No, I don't want to see either one of them," he fussed when I told him he had a routine appointment with one of these doctors.

As the illness advanced and his ability to verbalize dropped off, he often waged war against these doctors through body language.

When I told John, "Today you're going to go see Dr. Anderson, the internist," he would remain silent, as though he were processing the information. His brow would furrow. His lips would pucker. His face would flush red. After a pause of maybe fifteen or twenty seconds, he would storm, "No!"

He would then start pacing—into the living room, into his study, into the kitchen, then the family room, sometimes upstairs, downstairs—anywhere, just to escape the reality of having to go to this person who had so diminished him.

Sometimes he refused to walk out the front door. I would open it, he would slam it shut. If I did manage to get him to the car, he sometimes refused to step into it. Other times, when I opened the car door, he slammed it shut to signal his continued displeasure.

After a few episodes like this, I switched John's care exclusively to Dr. Demetrius, a specialist in diseases of the elderly. John liked him. Even with his growing disability, John remembered that this doctor was not associated with the car license debacle.

Once when I told him, "Today we're going to see Dr. Demetrius," he replied, "The sooner the better."

"How are you today, John?" Dr. Demetrius always asked. Then he would wait patiently, often many moments, until John could piece together a response; sometimes he could say nothing at all.

"Do you feel pain, John?" Dr. Demetrius would then inquire. Again he would wait for a reply. On one occasion, John shot back, "Of course, I do."

Dr. Demetrius understood that his patient's real identity extended beyond mere medical-scientific classifications.

$\mathcal{I}$n the old days, office paperwork occupied John after dinner. Now action-packed videos, especially stories about World War II, like

Stalag 17 and *The Great Escape,* were his entertainment of choice. Nothing gripped him more than the movie *Anastasia.* He sat through it without interruption. At its end, he said, "Quite a story!"

Why did these subjects captivate him? They seemed to reflect highly charged emotional events from his life, such as his years in the army. And maybe long-term memory still served him better than short-term memory.

*A*bout four months after the diagnosis, John asked me after dinner one night, "May I have a wooden finger?" Since by then I had begun to piece together the pathology of dementia, I replied, "You mean a toothpick?"

"Yes," he replied, grateful that I had understood.

One day he tried to shave himself with a flashlight. On another occasion, as he prepared to go to work, he put on his underpants, then his pajamas, then a pair of trousers, and then still another pair of trousers. One night, he came to my bedroom in the middle of the night crying, "This is an emergency!" When I turned on the light, I saw that he had put his legs through the arms of a long-sleeved shirt. He was trapped as if in a straitjacket.

Agree with everything. Never diminish him. I tried to remember earlier training.

He grew increasingly nocturnal. On some diabolical nights he was like one possessed. Lights flickered, objects crashed, doors slammed, and TVs blared.

He undressed himself until he stood naked, shivering in the cold. He stripped his bed. He emptied his closet. He unloaded his chest of drawers.

During some of these nights his resources were so diminished that he could not call my name for help. He didn't *know* my name. But names didn't matter. Names are about civilization. This was *beyond* civilization. It was primeval.

A nurse later tried to explain John's irrational behavior. "John was a go-getter all his life. Wherever he was, he had to go to work."

Indeed, during his well years, he was a workaholic. He was always focused, always driven. Now, as his brain became increasingly victimized by this plague called Alzheimer's, but with his innate drive still somehow intact, his overt behavior often manifested in a busy madness.

John was the son of immigrants from Brittany—that lonely French peninsula that juts unevenly into the Atlantic Ocean. For a time Brittany was an independent duchy, but after the French Revolution it became just another French province. Because of its remoteness, France took few initiatives on its behalf. Its economy stagnated, causing young people to emigrate in droves. Around 1900, John's parents were among them, eventually making their way to the U.S. and the Pacific Northwest.

John worked his way through college, dropping out after his junior year to save enough money to complete his senior year. Yet he graduated Phi Beta Kappa and became a first alternate for a Rhodes Scholarship.

Naively, I have always believed that excellent people deserve excellent deaths. *The quiet dying in one's sleep. An instantaneous heart attack. A quick fatal blow.* I was a dreamer. Still, I wanted some of the excellence of John's life to pervade his dying. My only recourse was to wrap his grim malaise in a cloak of dignity.

With the growing firestorm at home, I decided to leave my job with the universities to freelance on a part-time basis. I didn't realize then that within another four months, I would have to stop working altogether.

*I*t was December, six months after the neurologist had diagnosed Alzheimer's.

"Do you hear human voices coming out of the dishwasher?" John asked me one evening in the Christmas season as I was clearing up after dinner.

"No, I don't. Do you?"

"Yes. They're very musical."

Sometime before he had told me, "There are spirits in your bedroom—good spirits—usually three or four—who help you."

To test his consistency, I would sometimes ask, "Is there a spirit in this room right now?"

"Yes, right over there," he would say calmly, while pointing to a corner of the room.

John's neurologist called it "hallucination." I wondered if it were something more.

By year's end, I had not yet realized that John's diseased brain could no longer differentiate between food and the brown soil in the potted plant on the supper table. At Christmastime I had placed a bright pink poinsettia at the center of the table. One evening I stepped away briefly and returned to find him spooning potting soil into his mouth.

"No, John!" I cried, horrified by the possibility that he might already have swallowed some of it. I reached into his mouth to extract the spoon-size dollop of dirt. So as not to emphasize deprivation, I quickly placed a dish of chocolate ice cream before him. Then to quell any sense of alarm, I hugged him and said, "Everything is fine and I love you very much."

*J*ohn's capabilities had eroded grievously and I had begun to think that I was in Dante's second circle of hell. The only ray of light during these bleak months was the occasional sweetness of John's dependency, his childlike quality, his trust, his gratitude when he kissed my hand as if to say, "Thank you."

When I asked him once, "Do you miss your mother?" he answered matter-of-factly, "Not at all. You've replaced her."

*B*ut these first six months after the diagnosis were just a prelude to what lay ahead; the twelve months that followed were the hardest of John's long slide into oblivion. They marked his first year of his severe dependency; he could no longer be unattended even for a moment. He was often awake twenty to twenty-two hours a day engaging in activities that made little sense: pacing, roaming, racing upstairs and downstairs and indoors and outdoors, dressing and undressing, displaying bursts of frustration—even anger—beating with clenched fists anything that didn't move. Maybe on some level he was running away from, or raging against, the agony into which he had begun to descend.

I was exhausted by the crises and the uncertainty of what might happen next. And I was nearly undone by a crushing empathy for this brilliant man who, through some cruel twist of fate, had been robbed of his mind and was now fighting the battle of his life.

I knew that I could not go on without help. "One hour with an

Alzheimer's patient is like two or three hours with an unafflicted person," Dr. Demetrius told me solemnly.

I spent about sixteen hours a day caring for John. If I multiplied by the doctor's factor, I was putting in between thirty-two and forty-eight hours a day looking after an adult male who had the capabilities of a small child.

I knew that I had to make some decisions, and I made them quickly. I would give up my job for awhile. I would care for John at home. And without delay, I would look for professional caregivers to help me.

CHAPTER 5

Demons on Our Way

"I increasingly see my support-person activity as being a major
part of selfless service and therefore of my own spiritual growth,
a type of meditation in action, a type of compassion."
—KEN WILBER, *Grace and Grit*

*T*hree magical human beings entered our lives—three caregivers—no, three saints. They gave John what can only be described
as unqualified love. By the time they came to us, Dr. Demetrius had
told me, "All curative measures have been taken. What remains is
TLC." And from these three magnanimous souls, John got it in its
purest form.

I presented Andrew to John as a possible "driver." John still had some pride. To think—let alone discuss—the notion that a stranger would bathe, dress, and feed him, even at that stage of his decline, would have been humiliating, and with humiliation we ran the risk of a tantrum. "Do nothing that precipitates anger," Dr. Demetrius kept warning me.

"What's your program?" John asked Andrew cautiously.

"I'll help you with the driving. We'll get you down to the office and back home," Andrew said in broad, non-threatening terms.

John liked Andrew, I could tell. I saw no resistance. Only quiet, approving passivity.

Andrew agreed to start within a month.

Already in his sixties and semi-retired, Andrew could only work six hours a day Monday through Friday. With John's nighttime forays, I needed someone to look after him from midnight until 7 a.m. Andrew introduced us to Tony.

Even with the help of Andrew and Tony, the strain continued to be great. I had recurring bouts of flu and pneumonia. I knew I had to find someone who could help me on Saturdays and Sundays. Enter our third caregiver, Paul, whom we found through an employment agency.

If the ordeal that followed had a silver lining, it was my experience with these three men.

Take Andrew, for example. Sophisticated and witty, Andrew had taste and style that far surpassed mine. Whenever I had a social issue—"Should we send flowers or just a note on the death of Elizabeth Barnes?"—Andrew would arbitrate like a White House social secretary: "Let's send flowers." Whenever I had a problem with decor, dress, or even what to serve for a special occasion, I would check with Andrew. "I'm having Reba and Julie over for lunch on Thursday. What would be a good and easy menu?" "Puff pastry filled with shrimp and salmon lox," the oracle fired back. And then there was the matter of how I decorated the living room. For several months after Andrew came to us he said nothing, but then one day after we had become friends, he said, "Rose Marie, I just can't see this living room anymore." With deft hands, he moved two or three pieces around the room, transforming the space in minutes.

As an English literature major in college, I had studied English history and been interested in the British monarchy. Whether it was my early training or just a penchant for gossip, I, like many others in the early 1990s, was caught up in the saga of the troubled House of Windsor. As an Australian who for years had lived in London, Andrew seemed to be my own personal pipeline to Buckingham Palace, supplying me with analyses and sometimes juicy tidbits that would have made even *People* magazine salivate.

With Andrew each weekday, John was the proper businessman making his way to Seattle's financial district, but in my eyes, Tony and John were the "party boys." With Tony, who worked the night shift, John played. Each night Tony arrived with bundles of food delicacies—smoked salmon, Häagen-Dazs ice cream—over which John happily idled during much of the night. Tony was our painter with a heart as wide as the Mississippi. He promoted his art when he wasn't looking after John. Tony knew God, and together he and John practiced a deep spirituality.

As an Eastern European in the United States to study computer science, Paul was our world traveler. Russia, Siberia, Greece were as familiar to him as Tacoma might be to a Seattleite. He wove tales about his adventurous life as engaging as any out of a sultan's bedchamber.

Thus in various shifts around the clock, Andrew, Tony, Paul, and I assumed the burden of looking after John as his decline became more precipitous. We became a family, the caregivers and I, with John our child.

"Why don't you put John into an institution?" a former colleague, Connie, asked me one day in the market.

"At this point, we can still manage," I told her. After catching my breath, I added, "If ever a man loved his home, it's John. He built it. His dad put the roof on it. It's his castle. And when John can still articulate his wishes, he tells me with much labor, 'Stay home. Stay home.' I know what he means and I know about nursing homes."

For me, home-centered dying might well be a cultural predisposition. During my years with my German grandparents, they exposed me to time-honored, old-world traditions, among them that birth and death should occur at home. Opa was born in 1878 and Oma in 1888, when it was considered heartless to put a revered elder into an institution.

They both died at home in the care of family members.

An acquaintance, Ginger, whose intentions were perhaps good, but whose words seemed harsh, commented casually, "A lot of people in your situation just put them into nursing homes, divorce them, and get on with their lives."

I was aghast.

Divorce was never an option.

For one thing, I loved John. And the more I witnessed his courageous struggle to hang on to old realities—the more I saw his child-like trust that somehow fate had placed him into responsible hands—the more I loved him. Who could abandon such a man?

*D*uring much of that first year of complete dependency, John took unusual pleasure in shredding tissue paper. For more than an hour at a time, he sat at the kitchen table tearing Kleenex into tiny fragments. I welcomed this activity, because it kept him quiet and in one place for awhile.

On the freeway to and from the office, John liked to pull the car's emergency hand brake. Other times while traveling at high speed on I-5, he threw open the car door as though to jump out. More than once Andrew had to pull off the highway to settle John down enough to continue home.

John had a love/hate relationship with Andrew. Sometimes he referred to him as "my financial advisor"; other times, as instigating a "hostile takeover."

As Andrew and John traveled the roads of Seattle, assorted topics of conversation spilled from John's lips—among them, surprisingly, the subject of death. With me he had nearly always skirted any mention of death, but now, with his censors down, he readily observed to Andrew: "I don't have many months to live."

"John, you could well have quite a long time yet to live."

But John was adamant. Soon after he said, "You know I'm dead, don't you?"

"No, John, you aren't dead yet. You're still alive," Andrew answered gently.

On still another occasion as they drove through a shopping-mall parking lot, John noted, "All these people are dead, aren't they?"

"No, John, they're very much alive," Andrew tried to convince him.

$\mathcal{U}$p to this time, I had rarely seen any violence in John. This was about to change.

One afternoon I came home and found that John had gathered butcher knives from kitchen drawers to build his own cache of weapons. He used one of these knives to come after a temporary woman caregiver.

John did not like her. He was by this time incontinent and afraid that she might change his diaper. Maybe in his atrophied brain the knife seemed a primitive solution to ridding himself of a threat. He didn't hurt the woman, but I later learned she was adamant about never working for us again. After this incident, I hid all but the most innocuous kitchen knives in a trunk where I was certain he would not look.

$\mathcal{A}$fter my stepfather died in Germany, I invited my mother to spend some time with us in Seattle.

"When are you leaving?" John asked my mother the moment she arrived.

"In a few days," my mother answered patiently, amused by his directness.

John listened to her response passively, but seemed by then to have already forgotten that he had asked the question.

John disliked company. It disrupted his routine. It diverted my attention from him.

Annoyed by her visit, and maybe in a primitive act of retaliation for my having brought her into his space, he grabbed me by the shoulders one day and smashed me against a kitchen wall.

In the past he had punched me mildly. He had pinched me, and once he bit me. But smashing me up against a wall—that was new.

"You hurt me, John," I cried in exaggerated anguish. "You make me feel sad."

He rushed to me, took my hand, and kissed it. Then his pursed lips relaxed. His sulky demeanor gave way to trust and warmth. We embraced.

"I love you, John," I said.

"I love you, too," he murmured in a speech that was by now almost always slurred.

When the behavior of this person who was once my husband became truly unfamiliar, Dr. Demetrius attempted to console me by saying, "He's now in his terrible twos. He's going through life in reverse and you're a single mom."

"Let him have his lucid moments," Dr. Demetrius added when I asked him about behavior-controlling medication.

And lucid moments he had. They came like currents from the deep, unannounced. On one such lucid day, I asked John, "How are you doing?" With complete acuity he answered, "Sometimes it's hard to go on." To that same question on another occasion he replied, "I'm tired of the school of pain."

When I told Dr. Demetrius about John's brilliant flashes, he said, "John has a phenomenal mind. There's a lot still in reserve that can come to the fore from time to time."

This hit home on an evening when I had a migraine headache. I asked Tony to rub my neck in the family room where John sat in his recliner. During the brief neck rub, John said nothing, but as Tony took him upstairs to the bedroom, John said to him, "I don't want you to rub her neck. After all, she is my wife."

Soon after, I went on a brief trip. On the evening of my return home, John came to my bedroom, ostensibly, I thought, just to look in on me. He was, by then, wobbly on his feet and Tony hovered a few feet away. John sidled up to me and whispered, "How can I make love to you with him around?"

On Christmas Day 1992, John's sons took him to be with them and their mother for holiday festivities, leaving me to my own devices.

I was simply not invited. In retrospect, I realized that not being included was the family's oblique Christmas gift to me, which I was then too run down and exhausted to comprehend. But I was amazed at John's astonishing grasp of the dynamics of the moment. Just as John and Andrew were leaving for the festivities, John turned to me and said, "What about you?"

"I wasn't invited," I said, trying to keep a brave face. "You go to the celebration with Andrew. I'll see you later."

"We're not that kind of people," John stormed as he shuffled obediently out the door on Andrew's arm.

After John and Andrew left, my armor dissolved and I collapsed into self-pity, a state that had become all-too-frequent lately.

"Okay, don't invite me," I sobbed as I watched the car pull away.

From my black hole of despair, I eventually heard a faint whisper reminding me that we have a choice in how we react to situations in our lives. We can be victims or we can reach out to life.

I called Margaret, a close friend, and said, "I'm going to be alone today—Christmas—is there any chance I can drop by with a gift for you and the children?"

"Drop by?" she screeched. "Come for dinner!"

Then Sarah invited me to join her family for dessert, and Sam and Marie asked me to stop in for a drink.

Suddenly, Christmas Day was filled. I was jubilant. John's children had given me a gift. They had set me free. For a few hours I was unencumbered. I could live. I could be myself.

Thank you.

$\mathcal{D}$uring this time, I cared for John eight hours a day. From four in the afternoon to midnight, we had our time to be alone.

On good days, these hours consisted of a nap from four to six, dinner from six to eight, videos from eight to nine-thirty, and bedtime at ten. Then prayers.

John liked to pray. They went something like this:

ROSE MARIE: "The Lord is my shepherd;"
JOHN: ". . . Lord . . . shepherd;"
ROSE MARIE: "I shall not want."
JOHN: ". . . want."
ROSE MARIE: "He maketh me to lie down in green pastures;"
JOHN: ". . . . pastures;"
ROSE MARIE: "He leadeth me beside the still waters."
JOHN: " . . . leadeth . . . "

ROSE MARIE: "He restoreth my soul;"
JOHN: ". . . soul."

John always persevered, doing his best until the end:

ROSE MARIE: ". . . Amen."
JOHN: ". . . Amen."

But not all shifts were that easy. Sometimes John was hyperactive, irrational, restless, and combative—so much so that I would have to call Tony, the night shift caregiver, to come in early to relieve me.

Usually, within an hour, faithful Tony appeared, ready to take on the dragon. I would then slog up to my bedroom, appalled at what had become of my life.

How can I ever find joy again . . . walk in the sun . . . laugh with friends . . . toast the sunset . . . be transported by beauty? My life is flat and dark, tasteless and arid, and I have no hope of its ever being otherwise . . .

Migraine headaches, insomnia, and fits of sobbing over such things as an unbalanced checkbook had become commonplace. They prompted my doctor to tell me, "It's time, Rose Marie, to let professional caregivers look after John exclusively."

Finally, I agreed.

With that, my role became that of facilitator. I helped the caregivers and spent hours with John, who had become a desperate, needy, clingy little boy. I was his "Mommy"—his everything.

"You are so good," he said to me one evening as I tied his shoelaces.

It was one of those lucid moments, when treasure washed up on a barren beach. Mark Twain said: "I could live on a good compliment for two months."

I lived on John's for years.

CHAPTER 6

Inferno

> "To handle tragedy may, indeed, be the mark of an educated
> man or woman, for one of the principal goals of education
> must be to prepare for failure."
> —VICE ADMIRAL JAMES B. STOCKDALE,
> *A Vietnam Experience*

According to his doctors, John was not supposed to live into his second and third year after diagnosis, but like a warrior on horseback, he rode bravely into each new phase of his decline.

When I challenged his doctors about their miscalculated forecasts, as one they said, "Yes, John is still alive, but only because of the excellent care he gets at home."

In spite of his relentless slide into cerebral atrophy, John continued to have amazing moments of clarity, when communication between brain cells seemed intact.

One evening as I pedaled away on my stationary bike, I said,

"John, I've now ridden my bike for five miles. How many more miles do I have to ride to make twenty?"

"Fifteen," he replied, without batting an eye.

But those moments were rare. Most of the time John was dreadfully confused. As I sat with him one evening, he casually said to me, "Please make some calls to locate my thirty-three Saint Bernards."

"Okay, John. I'll get on it right away."

My response pleased him. He settled back into his recliner with an air of accomplishment. He felt credible. People were still listening to him. It was a balm for what must have been by then a mangled ego.

"I never do anything right," he cried mournfully one day.

"Yes, you do," I insisted. "You're doing fine, John. I love you very much," I said softly as I hugged the shoulders of a frame that now carried only 140 pounds.

It was around this time that Mike Tyson was convicted of rape. John, a lifelong sports fan, caught fragments of the story from TV newscasts. *Tyson. Rape. Prison.*

On the day CNN announced that Tyson would indeed have to go to prison, John, ever one to live a clean and tidy life, told Andrew with great alarm, "I shuuuur hope that doesn't happen to me."

"John and I have been walking six hours straight," Paul moaned one afternoon when I returned from running errands.

"Have you tried to distract him with ice cream?"

"Yes, he won't even have any of that," Paul said in near defeat.

At times John knew that he was behaving madly. On one such peripatetic day, he cried out, "I am so sick and tired of walking in circles."

I was tired of the struggle, too. The word "institution" had slowly begun to tunnel into my mind.

The workload. The confusion. The exhaustion.

Then as always, I was overwhelmed by guilt. And always John had a way of rescuing me from my discouragement with one of his lucid moments.

In spite of having relinquished my hands-on caregiving responsibilities, my energy often just evaporated. Indeed, by now I was so tired that I began to wonder if I myself were in the early stages of Alzheimer's disease.

I would make lists of five things to do. I would accomplish the first two and then absentmindedly skip to the fifth. I began to lose things—my car keys, the house key. I overdrew my checking account. Uncharacteristically, I stopped hanging my clothes in my bedroom closet. For days at a time they piled up on a chair in one corner of the room. My bathroom was in chaos. I forgot to renew my car license tabs, finally ending up before a magistrate. I had trouble sleeping. One day I lost my balance and fell on a cement sidewalk, scraping both knees, my chin, and the palms of both hands. When I paid bills, I found myself addressing the payment back to us. My head blazed with migraines. Insomnia nearly drove me nuts. And the vomiting. I was like a bulimic, only I wasn't. I wanted to keep my food down, but I couldn't. For a time I was almost afraid to eat. I remember going to restaurants and eating only lettuce—no dressing—for fear of regurgitating my food.

I tried everything I could do to help myself. Exercise was one avenue of release. I joined a gym. I lifted weights. I ran. I walked. I practiced yoga and deep breathing exercises. I meditated in agitated fashion. I drank warm milk before bedtime to help me sleep. And always I sought God. I made pilgrimages to a large Seattle cathedral where I lighted votive candles, believing that this act might strengthen my petition to God. But the cathedral was also a magnet for tourists, and I felt increasingly conspicuous in my attempts at serious prayer. More and more, I turned to the simple splendor of our garden as my place of worship.

"Why, God?" I kept asking. "Why such a catastrophe? Is this supposed to be some grotesque test of faith, or, for those of us who witness John's suffering, some insane schooling?"

Often I felt God walk with me, prodding me to keep my heart open in spite of the pain that surrounded me. Sometimes, however, God seemed distant, so much so that one day I heard myself saying to my sister Anne, "I think God has forgotten me."

"No, He hasn't," she quickly replied. "There's so much good in your life." After a pause as if to assess how best to make contact with my tired, distraught mind, she added, "The presence of suffering doesn't mean that God's not around. It's just that His purpose is not always apparent, given our limited consciousness. Just know that you can get through this trial and that you can come out of it stronger than you were before."

At that moment in time, her wise words flew past me, missing their mark. I was hitting rock bottom.

I was shocked one evening when a friend said over dinner, "Rose Marie, you're talking about death too much."

"I'm living death," I said as tears streamed down my face.

Indeed, I had begun to think that if I didn't die when John did, I'd die soon thereafter. There came a time when it seemed senseless to buy new clothes.

I'll be dead pretty soon, so why bother?

I was so convinced of my impending death that I began to check out retirement homes—those with infirmaries. Not for John, but for me. Someplace to die after he died, where I wouldn't cause a ruckus for my family.

I was only fifty-three. To my horror, I learned that these retirement communities don't even admit people until the age of sixty-two.

Concerned that I was losing my grip, I consulted my internist whose subspecialty is neurology.

"Could I be in the early stages of Alzheimer's?" I fretted to my doctor of twenty years.

After a long conversation and some tests, he said, "You're fine. You're just overworked. You need to take more time off. You need to get out of the house at least one day a week. Try to get out of town for a few days every two or three months, and find yourself a counselor."

$\mathcal{M}$y counselor, Dr. Reynolds, encouraged me to acknowledge the gravity of what had happened, to talk about my fears, to cry when I needed to. He reminded me gently that compared to children or even adults in their early prime, John had been granted a long and rich life. At the turn of the last century, life expectancy was forty-seven to fifty years. Now it's more than seventy-five years. "Maybe it's just John's time." He referred me to the Book of Job, an account of loss and restitution, as a way of looking at *Why John?* or, for that matter, *Why me?*

He encouraged me to think about the joys in my life—my family, close friends, the kindnesses of strangers, even the memory of my life with John before he became sick. He had me recount the times in my life when I had felt loved. He suggested I celebrate anything that brings hope. "Visualize your future. Write about your dreams," he said again and again.

I told him that I dreamed of Italy—that I wanted to go there someday—that I didn't understand the pull of Florence.

"Buy a large map of Italy and tape it on your bedroom wall," he responded. "At night before bedtime, study it. Put a red circle around Florence. Visualize being there."

I did, and one day I bought a red jacket that I thought looked "Italian." To that I added Polo sunglasses and an Italian-language book.

Most helpful of all was Dr. Reynolds's suggestion that I read inspirational literature that would feed my starved inner life. He referred me to *In the Midst of Winter* whose editor, Mary Jane Moffat, writes, "Literature is one of the few resources we have for living the deep life and not being simply spectators of our own experience. Love, loss and death, of course, have always been its great themes."

I devoured the writings of Auschwitz survivor Viktor Frankl, especially his book *Man's Search for Meaning,* in which he wrote: "everything can be taken from man but one thing: the last of human freedoms—to choose one's own attitude in any given set of circumstances, to choose one's own way."

Ernest Hemingway gave me courage when he wrote in *A Farewell to Arms,* "The world breaks everyone and afterward many are strong in the broken places."

Rabbi Harold Kushner gave me hope in *When Bad Things Happen to Good People:* "Now that this has happened to me, what am I going to do about it?"

And Anne Morrow Lindbergh inspired me when she wrote in her book *Hour of Gold, Hour of Lead,* "But when all is said about the universality of tragedy and the long way out, what can be added to human knowledge or insight by another example? . . . I can only say that one is helped by learning how other people come through their trials. Certainly, I was strengthened by the personal experience of others.

Biography now seemed fascinating. What helped others cope? What was their secret? What was their genius? John Gunther's *Death Be Not Proud,* Robert and Suzanne Massie's *Journey,* and the collected writings of Vice Admiral James B. Stockdale gave me clues. The more I explored other people's answers, the more I wanted to process my own. I had always jotted notes in a diary, but now I began to record events more thoughtfully.

At first, shock and confusion spilled onto my pages. Then rage and exhaustion. But I kept on writing, determined to work my way through the emotional minefields. And the more I wrote, the more I realized that just as the ocean has its tidal rhythms, so does despair. We can integrate loss into our lives. Pain can refine us.

I tried to keep my experiences in perspective. I told myself that out of what I hoped would be a lifetime of at least eighty years, two, three, or even four years of intense service to another human being was a very short amount of time. I reminded myself that in spite of John's illness, I lived well. I wasn't in Auschwitz and I wasn't in the Gulag. If I needed more help in caring for him, I hired it. If I wanted a new dress, I bought it. If I needed a break, I took one. When all else failed, I knew that if conditions at home became truly unbearable, I could, indeed, place John in a nursing home. There were worse lives.

It was also during this time that women friends became a haven in the wilderness. Their gifts of experience, joy, sorrow, and even failure nourished me. My women friends' perspectives on their own journeys through loss into healing gave me courage. My sister Anne phoned regularly from Belgium. My mother came all the way from Germany to visit us. Few inspired me as much as Kim and Bobbi, both breast cancer survivors, who today are radiantly alive and creative women.

CHAPTER 7

A Falling Star

"It is good to grow wise under sorrow."
—AESCHYLUS, *The Eumenides*

May 12, 1993, started like any other day.

John had gone to the office with Andrew. They had come home for lunch. At one o'clock Andrew finished his shift and Bruce, a temporary caregiver, took over.

It was a lazy afternoon. John rested peacefully in his recliner in the family room that looked out onto a sea of rhododendron bushes.

With John resting, Bruce felt confident that he could step away for a moment to use the bathroom. Just then the phone rang. Instinctively, John jumped out of his recliner to go after the ringing sound. His leap was too sudden. He lost his balance and fell.

When Bruce returned to the family room, John was sprawled on the floor, crying out in pain.

Gently, Bruce picked John up and placed him back into his recliner. Certain that he was only shaken and not in need of a doctor, Bruce gave him Tylenol.

When I returned at three that afternoon from running errands, I noticed an unease about John that I had not seen before. He looked drawn. He was moaning.

Worried, I called the doctor, whose first question was, "Is John breathing normally?"

"Yes," I answered.

"Is he spitting up any blood?"

"No," I replied, relieved that he didn't have serious symptoms.

"Then it's probably just a bruise. Even if it were a cracked rib, we'd still keep him at home. Give him two Tylenol every four to six hours and let me know if anything changes."

The hours inched by. John continued to moan. He whimpered. I called the doctor again. "Keep up with the Tylenol. John's just going to have to tough it out."

For three days, the caregivers and I watched him doggedly. Intermittently, I called the doctor—as much for my benefit as John's. I was nervous about his condition, but as before, his breathing was normal and he was not spitting up blood. From the doctor's perspective, John was stable.

On the fourth day John's breathing grew labored. He started to run a low-grade fever. The doctor prescribed antibiotics.

As the day waned, his breathing grew even more labored. Again, I called the doctor, who said to stay calm and watch for further changes.

We put cold compresses on John's forehead, hoping that the cool cloth would alleviate some of his stress, and I probed for responses from him. I wanted to hear, "Yes, I feel okay," or "No, I feel terrible," or "It hurts right here." But he couldn't tell me his pain. His brain no longer produced enough of the chemical acetylcholine to transmit messages. He couldn't show me where it hurt. If love is an energy that can be willed to another person, mine was streaming to this burdened man.

Suddenly, loud rattling noises came from John's lungs. He was gasping for air.

I called the doctor again, who at that moment was not available.

By now on autopilot, I called 911.

Within minutes a bright red fire engine pulled up in front of our house and a team of medics began checking John over.

After listening to his lungs, one medic said to me, "He needs to go to the ER for proper evaluation."

In the hospital doctors found four broken ribs and pneumonia in one lung. He would have to be admitted.

Even in his childlike state of mind, John disliked hospitals. As they prepared to wheel him to the eighth floor of the large medical center, he grabbed my hand and said, "Am I going to die now?"

"No, John, but you are being admitted to the hospital. You have pneumonia, which they are going to try to cure with antibiotics."

Contrary to what others around me said, I continued to believe that John could still receive far more than he could give. Simple and honest explanations seemed to comfort him, as did human touch.

We held hands as he was wheeled upstairs. At short intervals I assured him, "John, you're going to be all right. You're just going to be here a couple of days while they try to arrest a spot of pneumonia in your left lung."

He looked at me trustingly.

Some weeks before when I had tried to engage him in conversation and at the same time to clarify how he now perceived me, I asked, "Am I your wife or your mother?"

"Mommy," he answered softly.

So as the gurney made its way through the labyrinth of the hospital corridors, up an elevator to a waiting hospital bed, I knew that to him I now represented the safety and reliability of a mother. And I played my role with pride.

Once settled in his room, the nurses began to administer his medication, and with that he relaxed.

I hated to leave him that night. In my overwrought state, I had begun to imagine that he could only stay alive through my sheer force of will, and then only if I hovered over him personally, but it was by now eleven o'clock and the nurses said he needed to rest.

$\mathcal{B}$y the next day, pneumonia had spread into both lungs. John was now near death. I called his sons and the minister.

"He probably won't make it through today," his attending physician announced on the fifth day of the crisis.

A death watch ensued, and with that, an indescribable feeling of loss swept over me.

My mind convulsed: *I know John is grievously ill . . . that pneumonia is an old man's friend . . . that for all practical purposes his mind is gone . . . that he's lived a good life . . . that Alzheimer's is an exercise in degradation . . . that everything that lives will eventually die . . . that it's through illness that we'll probably meet our end . . . that John has reached a respectable age. Yet, I don't want to lose him.*

I prayed to God, "Don't let him die."

"Why are you so obsessed with letting him live?" Connie asked when I told her about John's condition at the hospital.

"Because I still see in him a desire to live and he left no living will," I cried. "When the nurses and I ask him, 'Do you want to die?—Is this getting to be too much for you?' consistently and vehemently he answers, 'No!'"

Inside myself I screamed, *I'm not a murderess!*

With all my might, I willed John to live. I felt like a gatekeeper. I would not let death approach. I visualized a cocoon of white light around his bed. I imagined armies of angels pouring healing energies into him. I continued to pray.

Not long thereafter, John's doctor said encouragingly, "He'll live out the week."

A few days later we learned that he would also live out the second week. Eventually, his doctor said that John could be released to go home with skilled nursing care around the clock. But the ravages of his fractured bones and pneumonia left him an invalid, tragically unable to swallow without choking or aspirating.

While in the hospital he had lost an alarming amount of weight. His doctor presented us with an ethical dilemma. Should we insert a feeding tube, which goes through his nose into his stomach; should we insert a feeding tube directly into his stomach through a surgical slit called a gastrostomy; or should we let John die?

Knowing John's wish to continue living, we decided to insert the nasogastric feeding tube, a procedure less radical than the gastrostomy. Our hope was that within a few days and weeks, once the pneumonia was fully arrested, he could begin eating independently again.

I converted the family room into a hospital room. Even in his disabled state, I knew that John wanted to be in the heart of the home. He liked the kitchen area, its rattling dishwasher, nearby washer and dryer, the TV, and the comings and goings of caregivers through the kitchen door. Into this space we installed an automated hospital bed. Oxygen tanks stood nearby, as did the feeding pump.

This scene was framed by a large bay window that looked out over John's garden, the green lawn that he had seeded himself many years before, the rhododendron and camellia bushes, and what would in a few weeks be his burgeoning dahlia garden.

The garden became my symbol of life. In the midst of the dying that surrounded me, the garden was about living—birth, growth, beauty, and the temporary triumph over inevitable death. In the spring the plantlings were my babies; in the summer, my peers, in the prime of life; in the autumn, when they began to fade, my noble forebears who had begun to take the journey I would take someday as well.

For the next six long weeks, John battled the nasogastric feeding tube. He hated its cruel intrusion into his nose, down his throat and into his stomach. Instinctively, he pulled at it. On the fortieth day of its insertion, he finally succeeded in pulling it out of his nose, begging desperately, "No tube. No tube. No tube."

But still he could not eat by mouth without aspirating. Without this technological feeding, he would die. Several nurses tried to reinsert John's nasogastric tube. He fought them. He resisted. He screamed, "NO!" Finally, the supervising nurse said that they could not go against a patient's wishes.

John no longer had the resources to understand that the tube was there to save his life. He only knew that the tube was hell and, in his diminished way, wanted to eliminate the hell. Since the doctors and nurses said a more humane method of feeding him would, indeed, be through a gastrostomy, we ordered one.

The only constant during these first frantic weeks after his release from the hospital was the amount of love John received. Before, his affliction had seemed so open ended, so many years. Now his doctors had given us a time frame, three to six months, so each moment with him was all the more precious.

Soon God will release you, I thought as I watched him sleep. *I want the time that is left to be a gentle movement into grace, and I want to create an environment that will abet that process.*

Give him peace, I prayed silently.

Mostly, during these weeks, John had little but consciousness to give, but we proceeded in the belief that he could still receive. His caregivers and I did our best to ply him with beauty: gentle touch, gentle talk, and classical music. We positioned his bed to look into a forest of rhododendron bushes. When the windows were open, birds chattered and the sun massaged.

With John now at home and completely bedridden, I was always on call. Wherever I went I carried a pager, poised at every moment to rush to his side, knowing with all my heart that I wanted to be present when his soul left his body. I was rarely paged, but I must admit that I cherished my time at his bedside. As he improved ever so slightly, as he gained more consciousness, against all medical prognoses, to see his radiance when I appeared, to feel him clasp my hand in his as though that touch confirmed our connectedness as a couple and his connectedness to life—the possibility of these small indications of life dominated my waking hours. To experience his gratitude for simple gestures such as a caress, a kind word, a few moments of my time. To experience, ultimately, the privilege of lending comfort to a dying man.

During that painful summer and autumn, when his doctors and nurses continued to prophesy, "He will be dead by September," and then, "He will be dead by Thanksgiving," John continued to rally and to have amazing moments of clarity. Often he expressed affection. On one of those bright and cloudless summer days, he said to me, "I don't know what I would do without you." Then he took my hand and kissed it.

"The greatest fear that patients like John have," Dr. Demetrius told me one day, "is the fear of abandonment." Indeed, by that fall, when he often drifted in and out of consciousness, it was tempting to question whether or not it mattered if someone hovered at John's bedside every minute of the day. Yet more often than not, after we stepped out of his room, upon our return, anguished peals of, "Hello, hello," greeted us. Sometimes when we came back, he said, "Please don't go away." Once I heard him call indignantly, "Where is everybody?" Maybe in all stages of life, even those close to death, we have an immutable longing for contact.

"Oh, John," I sometimes asked, "Does any of this add up? Your anxiety? The turning, the prodding—the endless enemas, injections, and blood draws?"

Sometimes he gave me a clue. One day he said, "I need help. I want to get out of here." Another time he echoed this sentiment by saying forcefully, "I want to get out of here and as far away as possible." And once when I asked him, "Is the struggle getting to be too much for you?" he replied, "Yes, of course."

On one level I knew he was tired of the fight, but when we asked him to choose between life or death, he always opted for life. With his body now sustained daily by 1500 ccs of perfect nutrition, one of his nurses said, "He could live for a long time. It could be years."

John's visiting nurses never spoke to me about his condition in front of him. Whenever they had something to say, they signaled me to step out of the room. There they would go over a new development or a possible prognosis. On one of these days when I had been flagged out of John's hearing range, a nurse suggested, "John might be hanging around because of your attachment to him. Reassure him that you will be okay if he goes."

*H*ow gently we tended this cherished being. We shaved him daily. Sponged his body until it had the cast of fine silk. Washed his hair and trimmed his nails. We applied lotion to his now translucent skin. Daily we changed his hospital gown and sheets, which I insisted be white with blue trim.

"A silly fetish," I would sometimes murmur to John. "But you are a boy, so no sissy colors for you."

He took his ablutions well. It was only when his visiting nurse, Agnes, scrubbed between his toes that he inevitably reacted with cries of, "Murder, murder, murder"—words he reserved only for the most outrageous indignities. After one of these outbursts I asked Agnes, "Does it really matter if we scrub between his toes?"

"Yes," she exploded. "One of the first rules of good health is to take care of your skin." But Agnes was on duty infrequently. When she was off, we ignored the toes regimen. His peace mattered more.

Once when I was caressing his forehead with maybe too much affection, he said faintly but with love, "Be peaceful and quiet." John now needed tranquility to conclude his earthly business.

He hated to be moved onto his left side, the side on which he had broken his ribs. There he still experienced tenderness. His face would wrench; he would moan. "But if we don't turn you every hour and a half, you could develop bedsores, and they alone could take your life," I said to him softly. Only when he was finally on his back did he relax and sleep, even snore—a sign to us that this tormented man was temporarily at peace.

It was during this period of convalescence that I came across John's baby book. His mother, Henriette, bore him when she was thirty-eight, and she lovingly recorded his journey into life. In the winter of 1916, when he was just a few weeks old, she had removed a lock of his fine golden hair, wrapped it in waxed paper, and taped it to a page. On one of John's hair-trimming days, I collected a gray-white lock and taped it beside the old keepsake.

*E*ach day when I awoke, I raced downstairs to the family room where John lay. I had an agreement with the night caregiver that he would call me if there were even the slightest change in his condition. In spite of that agreement, I was always relieved when I saw for myself that, indeed, he was still with us. Typically, then, I would take his hand in mine and say, "Good morning, John. It's Rose Marie."

Long ago, John had set aside any sense of duty to interact with people, but one morning after I had said, "It's Rose Marie," he replied, "I know that," in a way that suggested he felt I was not giving him enough credit.

I often felt confused. On the one hand, his doctor said he was severely mentally impaired. On the other hand, from time to time he responded with such clarity that I felt lightning had struck my soul.

On some days when a nurse had to leave early or we simply had a few moments alone, I talked with him in a more substantive way. I told him how much I loved him and how much our time together had meant to me. I told him that I was so proud of all that he had achieved in his life and, even now, how courageously he conducted himself. And sometimes, as on earlier occasions, I added, "If this gets to be too much for you, close your eyes and go to sleep. Go be with the angels and with your mother Henriette and your father Philippe."

Only once did he respond to such a suggestion. In a tone that cried exhaustion, he whispered dimly, "Okay, tomorrow," as if today he wanted only to rest.

I sensed that John had overlooked executing a living will in his desire to put off the thought of dying. Ignoring reality had left us with the daunting task of making his life-and-death decisions for him. But I couldn't blame him; I had acted on the same blindness to reality when I failed to insist on a living will as part of our terms of marriage.

Before he became disabled, we had discussed death on several occasions, but nearly always in a detached and intellectual way. We talked of a discarding of the body, an emergence into a new form of life, a continued consciousness, an ongoing growth.

Knowing that he probably couldn't answer me, but that his soul was fully alive, one evening I asked, "John, do you remember our talk about the English poet William Wordsworth and his poem, 'Ode: Intimations of Immortality'?"

I read the lines about "trailing clouds of glory" that John had recited to me long ago when we were courting, when he had wanted to impress me with his knowledge of English literature. As I read, John's eyes looked to the ceiling with fierce concentration as if he were trying to put the words into some kind of context. Moments passed. Suddenly, a small hint of pleasure shone on his face. His mouth registered a faint smile. Something warm and approving passed between us. I sensed strongly that far more continued to enter his consciousness than was able to come out.

I prayed to God for John's peace, especially when he moaned and we had to administer morphine to ease the pain, or, more often, give him liquid Tylenol by syringe.

Why, God? I still asked silently.

Let me understand. What is it you want of John? What is it you want of me?

I want to help.

What more can I do?

Faith is sometimes a difficult leap. When Carl Jung was asked toward the end of his life if he believed in God, he replied, "I don't believe. I know." I wanted that kind of confidence.

Those who witness the passing from life to death report that the dying often appear to be given glimpses of the beyond. The overwhelming report is that death is not something to fear—that beauty, reunion with others who have gone on before, and a sense of love await us.

As my stepfather, an agnostic, lay dying, more than once he came to consciousness long enough to tell my mother, "I have been in ecstasy . . . the music, the light, the peace, the beauty . . . I want to tell the children."

Toward the end of John's life, he spent much of his time looking heavenward, seemingly blissful at what he saw. He did not want to be distracted from whatever passed in panoramic fashion before him. Perhaps he was glimpsing another world and those in it. When I asked him, "What do you see up there?" he remained silent. When I asked, "Do you see the angels up there?" he replied, "Yes."

At John's bedtime I continued to recite our prayers of old. To what degree this ritual held meaning for him now, I wasn't sure. But, as before, I believed that his soul consciousness was still intact.

Often I simply caressed him. I placed fresh flowers in a vase near

his head hoping that their fragrance would waft into his consciousness. And I played Mozart, Schubert, and Brahms. Still other times,
remembering how much he had loved to dance, I played music of his
era. The strains of Glenn Miller and Guy Lombardo often lilted
through our house.

Music sometimes carried me to other times and places. I remembered when John and I visited Sydney, Australia, years before and
went to Manley Beach. We were warned about shark attacks in
which 600- and 700-pounders came ashore killing people right on
the city beaches. Without even a thought, John had ventured into
these waters, "just to cool off."

"But John," I cried as I watched him take his first steps into the
teeming surf, "don't you know that sharks are known to attack in
knee-high water?"

He didn't care. Mr. Invincible. He was enraptured by the sun, the
waves, the freedom, the flow. He seemed to have passed into a magic
place, joining the elements, becoming a child again. Nothing could
harm him. I liked what I saw. This serious man, this achiever, briefly
unshackled, vibrating with the universe.

*I'm so glad he had those experiences. Maybe somewhere in his soul he
remembers these joys. Maybe somehow he can venture back into those
places of wonder where it's warm and safe, and he can be reminded of his
true identity.*

CHAPTER 8

Good Night, Sweet Prince

"All goes onward and outward . . . and nothing collapses,
And to die is different from what any one supposed,
and luckier."
—WALT WHITMAN, *Song of Myself*

John did not die within the three-to-six-months time frame pre-
dicted by his doctor in June 1993. He lingered through most of 1994.

In January the outer world held less and less interest for him. He
dozed more. He reacted less. My 1994 diary shows fewer entries con-
cerning his activities. He was detaching. When he did interact, it
was brief and deep.

In February John once again asked for connectedness. "Don't go
away," he murmured as I made overtures to leave his bedside to ful-
fill other tasks. Sensing his neediness, I took his hands in mine and
whispered, "I won't leave you, my angel. I'm with you all the way."

He gripped my fingers urgently, beseechingly. His eyes locked onto mine as though he wanted to fuse with me and thus with life.

I reassured him again, "You can count on me, John. Always."

Burdens seemed to fall away.

At that moment I knew I had no more important work than to be with him, to comfort him, to love him. Instinctively, I now understood that I was performing the most awesome work of my life.

I was loving another life unconditionally. I was serving. For brief moments, I felt a mysterious kinship with other servers who had gone before me. I felt the interconnection of things. I felt that the tiny tesserae of my life, those scattered, seemingly random events, were coming together into a wondrous mosaic that told one story, the story of love. I had been preparing for this assignment with John all my life. My sense of loss dissolved into gratitude that John had touched my life and that I had been able to serve in this way.

*D*uring much of 1994, I continued to explore spiritual writings, still hoping to find fresh perspectives on healing from others who had gone before me. By now I had exhausted the works of contemporary authors and had begun to look into those of other traditions and other ages.

Lines from Montaigne's essay "That to Philosophize Is to Learn to Die," which I read at this time, consoled me.

"Death is to be feared less than nothing."

"No one dies before his time. The time you leave behind was no more yours than that which passed before your birth."

"Make room for others as others have for you."

Montaigne quotes Lucretius: "Why, like a well-filled guest, not leave the feast of life?"

"The advantage of living is not measured by length, but by use; some men have lived long, and lived little."

"Go out of this world . . . as you entered it. The same passage that you made from death to life, without feeling or fright, make it again from life to death."

I also found solace in John Donne's poem "Death, Be Not Proud," especially the line "One short sleep past, we wake eternally."

But the work I kept coming back to was the book *Peace of Mind* by Rabbi Joshua Liebman. In chapter 7, "Intimations of Our Mortality," I found lines that seemed to have been written just for John and me. Among them was this:

> for each one of us the moment comes when the great nurse, death, takes man, the child, by the hand and quietly says, "It is time to go home. Night is coming. It is your bedtime, child of earth. Come; you're tired. Lie down at last in the quiet nursery of nature and sleep. Sleep well. The day is gone. Stars shine in the canopy of eternity."

When words of comfort failed me, and they often did, I would simply hold John's paralyzed fingers in mine. I would wrap my arms around his emaciated shoulders. I would put my head on his pillow to let him feel human closeness.

*E*ven though John's life had begun to flicker, I continued to be amazed by his moments of lucidity.

When returning from a respite, I called Andrew from the airport to say that I would be coming home by Shuttle Express. When John heard this, he said matter-of-factly to Andrew, "Why not by taxi?"

On Easter, I was invited out to dinner with old friends. Always before leaving for a social engagement, I went to John's bed to say goodbye. On this occasion I had put on a new spring dress. As I hugged and kissed him good-bye, out of the blue he said, "You look pretty." I sensed a sad resignation that he could not go with me.

On June 22, 1994, John gave me what I later realized was my farewell gift from him—my last real communication. On that bright June afternoon, as I held him gently, I suddenly heard a tortured and slurred, "Iaaahhh luuuuve youuuuuuu."

Shocked that John would still be able to say anything at all after nearly a dozen weeks of silence, and uncertain that I had heard him correctly, I said, "John, did you say you love me?"

"Iaaahhh shuuuur dooooo," he answered laboriously.

I was awestruck by his capacity to still receive and, in this case, also to give.

At that moment I felt I had been touched by God. My efforts had not been in vain. I felt a love and humility I had never before known.

The last word that John ever spoke to me occurred on the final day of August 1994, when I told him good night, hugging and kissing him before I went upstairs to bed.

To that he whispered a warm, but tired, "Night, 'night."

John was being borne away. Soon he would be carried on a great tide. He was making his peace. He was reaching his fulfillment.

*J*ohn's last week of life brought dramatic changes. He began to sink into a deep sleep. Only shallow breathing emanated from this shell of a man.

He's already with the angels, I liked to think, and only occasionally comes back to look in on us, maybe already floating in the ethers above me, passing into the realms of history. All that remains here is his body, tired, worn out, on the edge of life, ready for his passage to the other shore.

Even in dying he was still strikingly handsome, skin like alabaster and hair like snow.

On his last day, when his nurse said, "It's just a matter of hours," I called John's sons; they came for the final vigil, which, with all earthly conflicts set aside, was a vigil of love. Soft kisses, gentle words and touch. Sibelius's "The Swan of Tuonela" played in the background. Dahlias peeked over the windowsill as if to offer a final salute. All was peace, the mood reverent. We whispered. Each in our own way, we said, "A job well done. A life well lived." Remembering his request of "Please don't go away," I held his hands. I stroked his arms. I kissed his forehead. I whispered, "I love you—always —forever." Time stood still. In some ways I wanted to hasten time so that he could be free sooner; in other ways I wanted to slow it down so that I would have him longer. But John was no longer mine. He hadn't been for a long time. He was now God's. We were operating on God's terms, not mine. *Thy will be done. I must remember that.*

John's nurse monitored his breathing which, as the hours passed, grew fainter. My heart was sinking, but it was also rejoicing because soon this challenged man would be free. Sometimes his breathing paused briefly. With her stethoscope, his nurse rushed to listen to his chest, which moved hardly at all. The breathing resumed. Then it paused. Then it resumed. In cadence, our emotions fell and rose. At 4:45 p.m. his breathing stopped again. Once more his nurse listened with her stethoscope. This time the breathing had stopped for good. "It's over," the nurse said gently. John had begun his voyage home.

It was October, and nearly dark outside. The sun had passed over our hill, leaving only shadows. A breeze swept through the camellia and rhododendron bushes, now dormant for winter's slumber. A bold clamor of birds rested briefly in our yard, listening. The Romans believed that birds led human souls to heaven. *Maybe these birds will guide John's spirit home to God.*

Feelings exploded. Tears flooded. Years of pent-up emotions gushed as if from a broken dam.

It had taken me a long time to understand the high calling to which I had been summoned by walking with John through his long trial. And strangely, when I began to acknowledge it, when I began to see the sacredness of what I was doing, when I began to work with what was, rather than with what I wished there were, when I began to appreciate my fate and to grasp in some small way the harmony that surrounded me, then John began to let go. It had taken me a long time to see in everything, even John's painful journey, holiness in its purest form.

*F*or the first nights after John's death, I felt a dreadful void. But the void was eased by sleep. The insomnia that had stalked me evaporated as if by magic. But still the void. The emptiness. The longing.

I miss him. Not the poor creature he had become, but his essence: His spirit. His soul. The person he was.

Sensitive to my needs, friends took turns staying with me during this difficult time. Then came the brave-faced formalities of death. The autopsy proved, indeed, that John had had Alzheimer's disease. The public announcement. The cremation. The memorial service with its theme of thanksgiving that John had shared his life with us, and our fervent prayer that now he could rest in peace.

During these initial shock-filled days, I was strangely consumed with doubt about John's safety and whereabouts—even in death. Apparently, my caregiving years had so programmed me that even in his afterlife, I felt a need to look out for him. When I expressed my concern about John's safety and whereabouts to his minister, he replied, "John's home. Death is the homecoming of the soul."

"But where is *home?*" I asked. "And if he's *home,* where is it and what's he doing at this point of his transition?"

The minister referred me to various biblical quotations that spoke of life everlasting. When I studied these verses and the Bible on my own, I sensed again that while God promises eternal life, on some issues He simply asks for our faith.

Within ten days my strange anxiety dissipated. Either I had finally been able to let go or, indeed, John's soul had settled into wherever it had to go.

As time went on I found comfort in realizing that though they had passed away many decades ago, my grandparents still lived within me; I have never felt them to be very far away. We are bound by love, which is eternal, transcending time and space. My grandparents come to me in my dreams. They are in my thoughts and will linger for all time in my memory. They are constantly accessible to me. I trusted John would be, too.

PART III

HEALING

CHAPTER 9

Reinvesting in Life Again

"Even if you meet betrayal and disappointment along the way,
go forth again the very next day."
—MERLE SHAIN,
When Lovers Are Friends

"You've had years to prepare for John's death," an acquaintance told me impatiently a few weeks after John's funeral. "What are your plans?"

"I don't know. I need time to think," I said, still dazed by all that had happened and embarrassed that I could not be more decisive.

During John's dying, it had been relatively easy to talk with Dr. Reynolds about my future, because, in a way, I believed I had no future, that I would die soon and that this talking was a game. But now, confronted with the reality of John's death, I felt paralyzed. I could not mobilize myself to create a future.

Dr. Reynolds, with whom I met another time or two after John's services, said, "Don't force the pain away. Wait. Let it be what it has to be. This is all part of the journey to healing."

My paralysis, however, removed me from the fray. That helped me think. *How do you reclaim a life?*

During John's ordeal I had developed a gnawing sense of my own mortality. This brought a great urge to do the things I'd never done before. *I want to nurture neglected possibilities. I want to climb mountains and swim rivers. I want to kick open doors that have been long shut.*

I knew that whatever I did after John died, it would have to be lifegiving. The question now was how do I make this happen?

*A*s the days and weeks passed, uncertainty consumed me. *Are my horizons now permanently circumscribed?*

But with the start of the New Year (1995), images began to emerge. They started with the house. *I don't want to go on living here.* John had suffered in this house. He had died in it. It personified sadness. *I feel that if ever I'm to be reborn, it has to be in a new space.*

I have read that the walls of a house sometimes become imbued with the energy of its inhabitants, that houses can be colored by either joy or sorrow, depending on the experiences of those who live in it. Within nine months of John's death, I had sold the house to a young couple with a new baby. Their bright energies would soon seep into the sad walls, restoring their original light.

Slowly, more images appeared. It was increasingly clear that I wanted to leave Seattle for a while, to put distance between me and my recent past, and to view life from a different perspective.

I want to go to Europe and spend time with my relatives.

I want to go to Italy.

I got the catalog from my university consortium's Florence program, and Italy seemed to fit the bill: *Art History. Renaissance Italy. Florence of the Medici.* The list was vast and my mind danced with visions of Michelangelo.

Maybe I was just naturally predisposed toward things Italian.

Although born and raised in Germany, even as a child I knew about Italy. My maternal grandparents had honeymooned in Tuscany. Oma could speak some Italian and when I was a child she taught me to say a few simple Italian phrases. It was our secret language. When we didn't want Opa to know what we were talking about, we'd switch into Italian. Of course, he knew as much of the language as my grandmother, but he never let on.

"*Ciao, Nonna! Come stai?*" (Hi, Grandma, how are you?) I could say by the time I was three.

"*Benissimo, grazie,*" (Very well, thank you) she would always answer with exaggerated pride. "*E tu?*" (And you?)

I had learned a whole repertoire of answers to that question, but my favorite was, "*Benone.*" (Great!) I liked the rhythm of that word. *Be-no-ne.* It reminded me of the German word *Banane.* It was a soft word. It made me feel grown-up to use it. And, inevitably, it prompted my grandmother to respond with a buoyant and approving, "*Brava.*"

*A*s long as I can remember, I've known about Johann Wolfgang von Goethe's book entitled *Italienische Reise (Italian Journey),* the account of his one-year visit in Italy in 1787. My grandparents used to talk about it, and these conversations left me with the sense that Italy was a land of culture, art, and ideas. As I grew up I came to understand that in some circles an extended trip to Italy put the final polish on a well-rounded education.

As a European teenager, rebellions had fascinated me. I liked the notion that the people who now call themselves Italians had thrown off the limitations of the medieval world half a millennium ago. And they'd done it by unearthing forgotten ideas from ancient Greece and Rome, thereby initiating what we now call the Renaissance. They gave the Western world a whole new view of what men and women are capable of being. Once I got to college in America and took courses in English literature, I realized that not only the Germans carried on about Italy; the English did as well. In *The Life of Samuel Johnson, LL.D.,* James Boswell writes that his idol, Dr. Samuel Johnson, observed, "A man who has not been in Italy is always conscious of an inferiority." And in *Childe Harold's Pilgrimage,* Lord Byron notes that he became "dazzled drunk with beauty" there.

Yes. Maybe Italy would be the place for me.

So I called Father Martini, the director of the American university in Florence, to ask if he would consider admitting a recent widow in the middle portion of her life. Fortunately, he said yes.

*F*riends reacted to my plans variously. One said, "Are you brave!" Another said, "Why are you doing this?" Patty said, "If not now, then when?" Joe said, "What's the commercial value of this?"

My mother in Germany said, "If anything goes wrong, we'll come right down to get you." My sister Anne, who is fluent in Italian, wrote out in large block letters and told me to memorize, *Mi può aiutare, per favore? Devo telefonare a mia sorella in Belgio.* (Can you help me, please? I need to telephone my sister in Belgium.)

*B*y early in the summer of 1995 my affairs were in order. I had sold the house and decided not to buy another until after my return. I put my belongings into storage. For this transitional period in Seattle, I could rent a small, furnished apartment. I had updated my will and rented a post office box. I arranged to have my bills paid.

As these plans came together, I sometimes felt as if I were jumping off the face of the earth, but I was ready for a bold move. I knew that it is a risk to try new things, but a bigger risk to try nothing.

I descended on relatives in northern Europe. I visited Paris and eastern Europe. I went birdwatching in southern France. I climbed the Alps and swam in alpine lakes and rivers. I visited Bruges, Amsterdam, Geneva. I reveled in my freedom to make decisions, to walk in the rain, to sit in the sun, to inhale the wind, to watch a flight of birds—to exercise all my senses.

At the end of the summer, with the start of fall semester just days away, I took an overnight train from my mother's house in Germany to Florence.

It was a night of restless sleeping. The stops and starts. The passengers getting in and out. The border controls. The monotonous rhythm of the train wheels that pushed south on steel tracks. But the hours I spent awake were rewarded with nighttime glimpses of snow-capped peaks, gleaming lakes, and fertile plains. I saw the bright heavens and wondered if John and all the dead whom I have loved were out there somewhere. As the train hurtled south, at daybreak I saw a whole new landscape of spiraling cypresses, olive and fig groves, and terraced vineyards held in place with stone walls. Occasionally I saw castles and fortified villages that suggested earlier intercommunal strife. I saw well-tended fields of summer maize and barley that would feed cattle and chickens. In the soft glow of dawn, I tried to catch a glimpse of the Italian wildlife that I knew hid within these rolling hills—wild boar, foxes, and songbirds.

Eventually, our train rolled into a city bathed in light. It was Florence and journey's end—or maybe better said, journey's beginning.

CHAPTER 10

A Greedy, Lusty Sensualist

"The moment we let ourselves be touched by beauty, that part
of us which has been badly bruised or even shattered
by the events of life may begin to be revitalized."
—PIERO FERRUCCI, *What We May Be*

"We've got to find a lover for Rose Marie," I overheard the university's dean of students, Father Pietro, say conspiratorially to Father Martini, shortly after the start of fall semester.

Me? A lover?

My mind reeled as I caught a glimpse of the two Jesuit priests conferring in a corner of the art-filled lobby of the rusticated-stone Renaissance palazzo that now served as the university's Florence campus.

I can't even imagine, I thought to myself. *After what I've been through?* For a moment the thought of ever loving another man terrified me.

Before I could say, "Wait a minute," to well-meaning Father Pietro, Father Martini, replied astutely, "I don't think Rose Marie is ready."

*T*his place is like a fairy tale, I thought. I'm in a country that has seventy percent of the world's art, and in a city that has fifty percent of that art. I'm in a palazzo that dates to the fifteenth century and enrolled in a university run by Jesuits who want to find me a lover. Priests are getting really liberated!

I must confess that I was secretly pleased that it would even *occur* to anyone that I should have a lover again. Briefly my mind lingered on his remark and flirted with the idea. Something strong within me wanted to respond to Father Pietro with, ". . . maybe later."

But I only thought those thoughts because at that moment in time, September 1995, I wanted something bigger than a lover. I wanted life!

I want to touch the trees, smell the wind, and feel the rocks along the Arno River. I want to memorize each aspect of the Orsanmichele, the Bargello, the Palazzo Pitti. I want to be with the students—to be one of them, to soak in their effervescence. I want to immerse myself in the teachings of the faculty. I want to be electrified with new ideas.

Sometimes, as I walked along the Arno in Cascine Park, I thought about the graveyard scene in Thornton Wilder's *Our Town*, where Emily, the heroine, recently deceased from childbirth, asks to be allowed to revisit an ordinary day on earth. Her wish is granted, but the visit is too much for her. "I didn't realize . . . all that was going on and we never noticed," she said sadly. In the end Emily cries mournfully, "Oh, earth, you're too wonderful for anybody to realize you."

Since John's death I often found myself thinking about all the things he loved, and strangely, about all the things I loved but never acknowledged loving. Simple things. Like the rain. The stars. The moon. Things that are always there, but that I had taken for granted.

Now in Florence I wanted to be a greedy, lusty sensualist, a visual drunkard, a glutton for life. I wanted to luxuriate in all the images that passed before my eyes—images that spoke a language that needed no words. The language of beauty. The language of harmony. Little did I realize then, as I do now, how shriveled my senses had become during John's long dying, when all the colors seemed to fade into gray skies, white uniforms, water glasses, and ashen pallors, and how healing this rich, sensual banquet would be.

I want to be wide awake and fully present. I want to feel adrenalin surge through my body. I want to remember who I once was. Then, later, maybe, I'll talk to Father Pietro.

I began that surge of adrenalin in what I later dubbed Signora Bertucci's Boot Camp.

In my eagerness to experience Italian life to the fullest, I had made arrangements, while still in Seattle, to be placed with a local host family. An American acquaintance of mine who had lived in Florence for fifteen years, had cautioned against this plan. "When it works, it's marvelous; when it doesn't, it's sheer hell," he said. "Unless I knew everything about a family situation, I would avoid it." But I had refused to listen.

The week before classes were to begin, and with childlike antici-
pation, I had arrived at the Florence train station and taxied to the
Santa Croce district and my host family, the Bertuccis. They lived on
the second floor of a buff-colored apartment house just a block from
where Michelangelo had lived 500 years ago.

I was met at the apartment door by a small, plain-faced woman
who turned out to be the grandmother of the *famiglia*. Her gray hair
stretched into a tight knot behind her head, emphasizing her steel-
gray eyes and slightly mustached lip.

Signora Bertucci spoke not a word of English but bristled with
authority. She motioned me to my room, a barren space with a cot,
a wooden table covered with a blue oilcloth, and a closet. The room
was fine; it was the reception that got me.

Where's Italy's generous heart?

The room's singular attraction was a sun-flooded window from
which I saw blue sky, neighboring courtyards, and a playground surrounded by flame-shaped cypress trees. Directly outside my window
were clotheslines strung alongside the stucco building.

As I unpacked, a middle-aged, Mediterranean-looking woman,
Maria Bertucci, arrived. In broken English she told me that, in addition to her mother and me, this two-bedroom, one-bath apartment
would also be home to two young Swiss women hoping to perfect
their Italian.

"Ingrid and Krista will share one sleeping room," she said. "My
mother will sleep on the living room sofa."

"What about the bathroom in the morning when we're all scram-
bling to get ready for school?" I asked, already suspicious of what I
might hear.

"My mother uses the bathroom first—at 6:15. You may use it at
6:50, but you may only be in the bathroom fifteen minutes. If you
wash your hair, you dry it in your room."

"What time is breakfast?"

"7:50."

"And dinner?"

"7:30."

"Do you serve lunch?"

"Never. You must eat out."

Maria said that from now on, only Italian would be spoken in the apartment. As an afterthought she added, "The clotheslines outside your bedroom window will dry the laundry for two apartments—mine, a block away, and my mother's."

I calculated quickly and realized that "my" clotheslines would dry the sheets, towels, and personal laundry for eight women.

This was the army and I had arrived in boot camp.

But I'm not a quitter, I told myself. *I've got to give this a chance. I'm in Italy to separate myself for a while from old patterns and to embrace new ones.*

Oh, but how I wish I had my down comforter from home!

*A*fter dinner that first evening in the Bertucci home, my two well-scrubbed Swiss flatmates, Ingrid and Krista, both in their early twenties, sampled with me that great Italian pastime, the *passeggiata*, a stroll after dinner to view firsthand the outdoor museum that is Florence.

Through craggy but luminous side streets, we walked to the Duomo, the cathedral that many consider to be the heart of Florence, to see its well-lighted, neogothic, marble facade—*green marble from Prato, white from Carrara, and red from Maremma, or is it the other way around?*

On this evening hordes thronged the piazza, mingling, talking, laughing, seeing, and wanting to be seen. We marveled at Brunelleschi's brick dome, the largest dome of its time built without scaffolding. We gaped at the Campanile, the Baptistry, and Ghiberti's *Gates of Paradise,* and from there we strolled to Piazza della Signoria and the Ponte Vecchio, all closed to cars.

After we had viewed the key sights around the Duomo, I asked Ingrid and Krista, "Would you mind detouring briefly to help me find the university where I'm to report early in the morning?"

"Of course not," they said almost in unison.

With the help of a city map, we made our way to Via de' Tornabuoni and the austerely elegant Renaissance fortress that would be my academic home for the next semester. My eyes caught the palazzos's well-composed dimensions and geometric patterns, especially the evenly spaced semi-circular window arches. Instantly, I felt *I will be happy here.*

Before heading back to the Bertuccis, we stopped at a *gelateria* for a *sorbetto*, a silky smooth fruit puree in such flavors as raspberry, banana, and peach.

Once in my room, I arranged my few treasures from home. John's picture in its silver frame, which in Seattle had sat on his old baby grand piano, became the focal point of my decor. It was from 1988, shortly after our marriage, and he had just won a tennis tournament—dressed in white—tall, trim, graying, smiling broadly with his trophy.

Now he was a photo on my desk, the oilclothed table, with pens, pencils, and paper clips.

I had remembered to bring a stapler, but had forgotten a pencil sharpener, a hole punch, and a magnifying glass. *I will have to learn those words in Italian to even buy them in a local store,* I thought to myself. That night the task of assimilating even minimally into Italian life seemed formidable. *Maybe I've taken on too much too soon.*

As I studied John's picture, I wondered, *Is it good for me to pore over his image this way, conjuring up memories, brooding over what is no more?*

I consoled myself with Dr. Reynolds's words: "Surrender to your sorrow, Rose Marie. The only way out of grief is through it."

I feel lonely tonight. Homesick. This isn't a bed. It's a camping cot. I don't have enough covers. And the bathroom faucet is dripping. And the noise outside, the roaring motorini.

Most of all, the loneliness. I love the idea of home. That's why I signed up to live with a family. I wanted a warm and ebullient Italian family, but instead I get this dour grandmother who's in this just for the money.

It's humbling to be separated from the things I care about.

I miss John.

I miss home.

I feel tethered to nothing.

How can I ever heal this grief?

Tears soaked my pillow that night. I took comfort in knowing that in a few short hours I would enter the palazzo for my first day of classes.

*A*fter a troubled night, my alarm sounded just as the sun tipped the tall cypresses outside my bedroom window. The *motorini,* which roared until two in the morning, were once again revving their engines. I went through the signora's formal bathroom routine, grabbed a piece of toast in her kitchen, and hurried along one of Florence's many cobbled, medieval streets to reach the university by eight.

As I ascended the palazzo's grand winding stone staircase, I wondered about all the people who had walked these steps before me and those who would be walking with me this semester.

It was at the top of this grand staircase that I overheard Father Pietro say something about finding me a lover.

A shocking thought . . . But I'm late for class . . .

As I slipped into my seat, breathless, in *Aula* I (Lecture Hall I), Professor Eleanora Raffanelli was saying, "Florence is a portrait in miniature of Western European civilization . . . the Florentines helped forge the modern world."

It was the opening lecture of a course titled Introduction to Florence.

"Florence was first an Etruscan settlement," she was saying. "The Etruscans were the first major civilization in Italy and well established by 900 B.C. Originally, they came from Asia Minor to exploit the peninsula's mineral resources for trade with Greece."

As she spoke I looked around *Aula* I and noticed about three dozen well-groomed young heads, all mesmerized by Professor Raffanelli—her appearance (impeccably groomed, in a suit), her crisp English enunciation, her questioning *"Eh?"* which she used to solicit a response, and her *"Very important,"* a cue that what she'd been saying would be on the next test.

"After a major war with Rome in 395 B.C., the Etruscan civilization declined. In 59 B.C. Julius Caesar decided to turn a small Etruscan settlement along the Arno into a colony for Roman war veterans. Since the colony was established in the spring, Caesar named it Florentia, suggesting floral games or fields of flowers, a gesture believed to have been a good omen."

At the end of class, Professor Raffanelli handed out the first-quarter term paper topics. As I scanned the list, my eyes rested on Lorenzo the Magnificent, the poet, statesman, and model Renaissance man. *I want to learn more about him,* I thought.

After class, I walked down the grand staircase of the palazzo into the colonnaded courtyard, through reinforced front doors, and out onto Via de' Tornabuoni, the Fifth Avenue of Florence.

Giorgio, the building's amiable concierge, called after me. *"Buona sera,* Giorgio," I called back, delighted with his greeting. It made me feel as if I really belonged. But I was still puzzled as to why, in the early afternoon, some Italians already said "Good evening," instead of "Good day."

So much to learn.

Giorgio, olive-skinned with well-cropped straight black hair, was handsome in a fragile way. He was friendly, but discreetly so. His work was to guard the palazzo, to keep track of who came and went. Once we became better acquainted, after I had passed through his *portone* a few hundred times, he confided in broken English, "You look like Jessica Lange."

I liked that.

As I turned right toward the Arno, Florence lay before me like a city of gold. The buildings' colors ranged from deep oranges to subtle bronzes to soft yellows and pastel creams. I rooted through my purse for sunglasses.

As my eyes adjusted to the sunshine, I caught sight of another tantalizing vista—the elegant fashion shops lining Via de' Tornabuoni: Gucci, Armani, Valentino, Versace, Ferragamo.

Italian women wrote the book on style. It's almost a matter of national pride to *"fare una bella figura,"* to make a good appearance, yet they are discreet in what they show. In *The Stones of Florence,* Mary McCarthy wrote, "Consumption is not conspicuous here. An unwritten sumptuary law seems to govern outward display. The famous Florentine elegance . . . is characterized by austerity of line, simplicity, economy of effect. In this spare city, the rule of *nihil nimis* prevails."

As I walked along Via de' Tornabuoni, I paused often to peer at *la moda.* Fashions were so simple that sometimes I thought, *I could sew that.* I passed shop windows that proclaimed their specialties— *profumeria* (perfumery), *erboristeria* (herbalist). Other imposing doorways boasted signs saying *Albergo* (hotel). Still others advertised upscale *bar* where I could find *panini* (filled rolls) and *tramezzini* (sandwiches). Even a *libreria* (bookstore) hyped its products. When I came to Via degli Strozzi, I turned left to cross Piazza della Repubblica and on to Via del Corso Borgo degli Albizi, a dark medieval lane that zigzagged, almost forbiddingly, to where I lived.

Once on Via del Corso, the highlight of my trek to the Bertucci *appartamento* was a wonderful little church called Chiesa S. Maria de' Ricci, tucked neatly along a lane of shops. It always surprised me—an unexpected and intimate sanctuary rising out of a commercial wilderness, and a sharp contrast to Santa Maria del Fiore, the great cathedral of Florence, which seats 20,000 people and boldly reaches to the heavens just steps away. I often paused at the small *chiesa*. On some days concerts of Bach's high Baroque summoned overflow crowds and made it impossible to find a seat. But the stalwart stood outside savoring Bach's rich glory. In the book *Rossini* by Herbert Weinstock, Gioacchino Rossini is reported to have said, "If Beethoven is a prodigy of humanity . . . Bach is a miracle of God."

CHAPTER 11

The Medicis Had Balls

"Ancora imparo!" ("Yet I am learning!")
—MICHELANGELO,
*The Home Book of Proverbs, Maxims
and Familiar Phrases*

By the end of the first week of classes, my mind blazed with new ideas. Courses were taught in English, from Monday to Thursday noon. From Thursday afternoon until Sunday night, we were encouraged to experience Italian life, usually by going on well-organized student trips, but also by savoring Italy's succulent *cucina*. In a cooking class, separate from the university's curriculum, I had already learned how to make *gnocchi di patate e spinaci*.

And I was making new friends, noting that none of them lived with a local family. Kathleen from Ireland was finishing her dissertation on how beauty leads to goodness. Frazer, a math major, was in Italy to explore, among other things, Leonardo da Vinci's scientific investigations. And Patrick, a philosophy major, was studying Renaissance philosophy, especially the works of Marsilio Ficino. Other students were exploring economic integration of the European Union or comparative legal systems. Still others were studying art during their junior year abroad. And I? Filling in some gaps.

At times the response of some younger classmates to human anatomy as depicted in art, especially nudity, was so adolescent that Professor Raffanelli, who also taught art history, decided early in the semester to desensitize them with a frontal attack.

"Today we're going to talk about balls," she announced soon after the semester began.

Gasp!

To the sound of muffled snickers, she projected a slide of the Medici coat of arms with its six red balls on the classroom wall.

She then held up a copy of *The Agony and the Ecstasy*: "The famous American writer Irving Stone wrote in this book about Michelangelo's nude marble statue, *David*: 'He [Michelangelo] had never understood why the erogenous zone had been represented as unbeautiful. If God made man as the Bible said he had made Adam, would he have made the area of procreation something to hide, something vile? Perhaps man had perverted the uses thereof, as he had managed to pervert so much else on earth; but what did that have to do with his statue? That which had been despised, he would make godlike.'"

Professor Raffanelli then added firmly, "In this class nothing human is foreign to art, and what is art is sacred." She paused and stared straight at us. Quietly, she then added, "In Tuscany we have a saying: Ignorance is the enemy of art."

The class fell silent.

She then proceeded to discuss various theories about what the balls on the Medici coat of arms might represent.

She mentioned the six-times dented shield of Averado, the brave eighth-century Tuscan giant killer, from whom the Medicis might descend. She touched on the notion that the balls were pills (*medici* means doctors), or pawnbrokers' symbols.

"But on the street to this day, the opinion is that the balls simply represent courage, as in 'The Medicis had balls!'"

The youngsters' tittering now erupted into nervous giggles.

A somewhat older student, math major Frazer, was often frustrated at the antics of our younger schoolmates. He commented to me, "Their brains are knee deep in sperm."

Early in the semester I had heard reverent whispers about the "potters," as if they were some elite student corps—*maybe sculptors in the making—future Ghibertis or Donatellos?* Our program had all kinds of art majors, those strictly enrolled in the studies of the history of art, but also fledgling sculptors and painters.

One day Frazer clued me in. "The potters are the kids who like to take the overnight train to Amsterdam to get pot."

The ready availability of alcohol caused occasional run-ins with the law. I heard of a brawl at a disco called the Purple Garter. Another time a student, who had had too much to drink, pulled a knife on a Florence policeman. He landed in jail. In court, the judge, (clearly fed up with the escapades of some of the foreign students in town) gave the boy a choice: serious jail time or get out of the country within two hours. The kid promptly opted to get out of town. There ensued a mad scramble to retrieve his clothes from his hotel and get him on a flight to anywhere. With the help of saintlike Father Martini, the boy pulled it off. I suspect that later that evening the good padre retreated to his tiny, under-the-roof apartment in the palazzo with a bottle of well-aged red wine.

But these episodes were rare. To me my younger classmates seemed a gust of fresh air. To them I was an object of some fascination. That an "older person" would undertake something like this seemed a little odd but also "cool." Gloria, twenty-two, said, "A lot of people just talk about doing something like this, but you're actually doing it." And I overheard Jeremy, twenty-one, tell another student, "When I'm *that* old, I'm going to do what Rose Marie is doing."

I was one of ninety-six students, most of whom were in their early twenties. At fifty-five, I was the oldest of the bunch. Generally, age was not an issue, although, obviously, my life experience was different from theirs. And physically, while I was healthy and strong, I couldn't streak up mountains like they could. I couldn't disco until 3:30 in the morning night after night. *Maybe I could,* I told myself, *but I just don't want to.* And no matter how I struggled to look good for my age, I couldn't pass for one of them.

"She's staff!" Father Martini snapped once while we were traveling as a group to the Middle East and a border official looked askance at me among my junior peers.

$\mathcal{B}$y the middle of the second week, it was clear that my arrangement with the Bertuccis wasn't going to work. My room had become a crossroads of dripping and drying laundry. Without warning, the Signora or Maria would barge in either to collect dried laundry or hang out wet laundry. Occasionally I found my belongings moved—books repositioned, pictures relocated. When the Swiss students and I dared speak German, the only language we had in common, the Signora bellowed rebukes from the kitchen.

She had it in her mind that I should speak Italian with her from day one. I was enrolled in Beginning Italian, but in just a week of classes I had not yet learned enough to satisfy the signora. The more I didn't speak, the more agitated she became.

On my fourth day in her apartment, during breakfast, the Signora slammed toast on my plate and ordered Ingrid, who was more advanced in Italian than I, to tell me in German, "By dinnertime tonight you will know the name of every object on this table."

"*La for - chet - ta,*" the Signora said towering over me and pointing to the fork to the left of my plate.

"*Ripeta!*"

"*Il col - tel - lo,*" she said, directing my attention to the knife to the right of my plate.

"*Ripeta!*"

In a similarly strident manner, she then pointed out *il cucchiaio* (the spoon), *il piatto* (plate), and *il bicchiere* (glass) and other objects on *la tavola* (the table).

As if by her intensity she could force me to understand, the Signora grabbed me by the shoulders, looked at me with her steely eyes, and said shrilly, "*CA-PI-TO?*"

"*H*ome" was a combat zone. After ten stressful days, the Signora had worked herself into such a fit over my inability to speak suitable Italian that she threw my cup of tea onto the floor and jumped up and down in the spilled liquid, gesticulating madly and shouting frenzied words, most of which I couldn't understand.

"*Che disastro!*" she yelled with glazed eyes.

I was speechless. I ran to get Ingrid to help me translate. The two of us pieced together that the Signora felt I was a hopeless case, and that I would never be able to speak Italian.

For years I'd felt bullied by the irrational behavior brought on by John's brain disease. Now I was besieged by a madwoman. After having just spent years watching a human life crumble before me, anything less seemed too trivial to fight over. I decided then and there to move into a small *pensione* less than five minutes from the university, a place that Father Pietro had told me about. Within forty-eight hours I was gone.

Somehow the Signora and I parted on reasonable terms.

Through Maria, the Signora offered to fix a favorite Italian meal on my last evening in her house. She asked me what I would like. In my first days there, I would have answered "Anything. It doesn't matter." But slowly, my appetite was returning. I asked for *spaghetti alla puttanesca,* a dish, which years before, I had enjoyed with John in Lucca, a town in northern Tuscany. I remembered John's taste for olives and his delight in how generously the chef had used them in our dish that day. I remembered, too, the dry white wine, Montecarlo, produced just east of Lucca, which John had ordered to go along with the *puttanesca.* The signora's version of this favorite dish didn't quite compare with what I remembered from Lucca years before, but it was a generous parting gesture.

I labored a halting, "*È molto buono, grazie.*"

The Signora nodded as if recognizing my attempt at Italian. She smiled slightly.

The morning after the farewell dinner with the Signora, I gave her a bouquet of flowers.

"*Troppo gentile,*" she said.

CHAPTER 12

We Will Be Your Family

"Just having a caring environment in which you can express
your feelings and be heard and accepted for who you are
is profoundly healing."
—JON KABAT-ZINN,
The Power of Meditation and Prayer

Once again my landlady was an aging signora, but this time a joy-
ful one who quickly dispensed with formalities, insisting that I call
her Teresa. Almost from the start, Teresa called me Rosa.

Stout but shapely, Teresa owned two *pensioni* in Florence, kept her
own books, and typed up a storm. Along with French and Spanish,
she spoke some English and German. With her language skills and
my humble Italian, we soon became fast friends.

Before I arrived, Father Pietro had told Teresa about my mishap with the Bertuccis. Whether he had told her about John's death, I was unsure. On the first day in her *pensione,* Teresa announced to me, "While you are in Florence, we will be your family." And that is how it was.

That I came to Teresa's *pensione* under Father Pietro's auspices was a distinct advantage. Teresa, sixty-four, was a devout Roman Catholic and, as one of Father Pietro's charges, I was instantly among the anointed in her eyes, indeed, almost infallible.

In the morning, the third floor of Teresa's *pensione* lobby resembled a circus. Telephones blared. Fax machines ground. The ever-unpredictable elevator clanked. Harried tourists barked. Marianna, the maid, dragging furiously on her cigarette, complained. And Salvatore, aged eighty, Teresa's long-suffering and Walter Mitty-like husband and handyman, begged for her attention. (Another age-discrepant marriage!)

Throughout, Teresa sat Buddha-like, dealing with the chaos item by item.

"*Marianna, comincia con la camera sette,*" ("Marianna, begin with room number 7") Teresa told Marianna, who, while waiting, had started her second cigarette. The faster she got through cleaning her assigned rooms, the faster she could be on her bus home.

"*Herr Schmidt, hier ist Ihre Rechnung*" (Mr. Schmidt, here is your bill") Teresa intoned, aware that this guest did not like to wait his turn.

"*Je vous conseille le petit restaurant au coin, Mademoiselle,*" (I recommend the small restaurant on the corner"), Teresa proposed to a young student from Lyon, France.

Even at sixty-four, Teresa's brown eyes still danced with life. Her gray hair fell softly into a chignon at the base of her neck. She didn't have the chiseled look of many of the other Florentine women, but style was not her forte. Teresa was a businesswoman. She owned two prime-location buildings in central Florence. Her *pensioni* only occupied two, at most three, floors in each of her multistoried structures. She was a landlord and collected hefty rents.

"I am very rich," she told me once after we became friends. What she did with her money, I don't know. From what I could see, she reinvested only the minimum into her properties. (Frazer referred to Teresa's *pensione* as "a one-star on a good day.") Occasionally, Teresa talked about her country home near Livorno and her part interest in a Chianti vineyard. Yet tourists flocked to her, whether the facility was well maintained or not. It had a central location and it was cheap.

*A*fternoons in Teresa's lobby flowed more easily than mornings. It was *riposino* time. Most of her guests were young enough not to want to waste time resting. But we infrequent older guests happily paused in the afternoon, if not for a *riposo*, then for a cup of coffee.

"Espresso, Rosa?" Teresa suggested one afternoon as I passed through her lobby on my way from class.

"*Sì, grazie,*" I answered preferring a cappuccino but feeling reluctant to make a fuss. I had already learned that in Italy coffee is a traditional practice, a prelude to further interaction.

I crashed into a frayed easychair near her desk.

"*Come sta?*" Teresa called from the adjacent kitchen where the hiss of the espresso machine filled the air with the thick aroma of coffee.

"*Bene grazie, e Lei?*"

I was pleased that, slowly, I was piecing some Italian together.

"*Non c'è male, grazie,*" she called as I heard jangling dishes.

As I waited for Teresa to return, my eyes ran across the

well-scrubbed marble floor. I could still smell the antiseptic that
Marianna had used in the scrub water that morning. To the left of
my chair, the wall clock ticked softly. And directly across from me
and in a easy rhythm, Teresa's homemade chintz curtains swayed
gently in an afternoon breeze. All of the windows in her *pensione* had
wooden louvers that diffused the rays of the relentless sun.

I had wanted to get to know Teresa, and was pleased that she had
invited me into her domain.

She sauntered back with two *caffè lunghi* (generous portions of
espresso) and sank into a second chair in the sitting area of her
lobby.

"Ah, che bello rilassarsi un attimo." (Oh, how nice to rest for a short
moment.)

Once seated, Teresa pulled her knitting from a side table.

"What are you making?" I asked.

"A vest for Salvatore," she answered proudly as her needles began
to whirl, clicking in even rhythm as she interlocked chocolate brown
yarn, pulling it forward, casting it off, and adding stitches without
even a thought.

As Teresa's fingers danced, we prattled. Business was good. No
vacancies. Constant requests for future reservations. Young people
are too noisy. Germans are obnoxious; they act like they own the
place. Taxes in Italy are a nightmare. The convoluted system. An
outrage! The influx of illegal immigrants! And my school work. How
was I doing? We discussed Padre Pietro. Teresa washes his laundry.
It's a privilege to look after a priest.

Occasionally the phone rang. Each time, Teresa pulled her tired
body out of the chair and lumbered to her reception desk to arrest
the abrasive sound.

"Have you thought of getting a cordless phone?" I asked after the
second interruption.

"Troppo complicato!" Teresa said with a dismissive wave of her hand.

Teresa was not into technology. A telephone and fax, yes, but nothing else newfangled, certainly not a computer. She maintained all her ledgers by hand.

Wanting to draw Teresa out, I asked, "Do you have any children?"

Teresa paused, looking up from her espresso with a mild squint in her eyes. She seemed conflicted about how to answer my question. Then she replied, "No, I have a man."

This probably means that her "child" is Salvatore, who's usually running around with hammer and nails repairing things.

Just as I began to think that I'd best not pursue this possibly sensitive line of conversation, Teresa continued, "I have a son, Alfonso, who is thirty-five years old."

I smiled as I realized that Teresa's and my communication would be very literal.

Of course she doesn't have any children anymore, I thought to myself. *She's too old for that. The one child she did have is now a man.*

With that simple question about children, Teresa's emotional floodgates opened. She could not contain herself. At every opportunity she shared still another revelation about Alfonso.

"This is Alfonso at his confirmation," she proclaimed as she pointed to a picture of an adolescent boy dressed in white.

"And this is Alfonso's wedding to Francesca." I saw a handsome, dark-haired man standing next to a beautiful bride in a flowing white gown.

"And this," she said, beaming brightly, "is Fabrizio, my grandson, who is now four years old." A curly-headed boy in shorts drinking out of a garden hose on a warm summer day mugged happily for the camera.

"Fabrizio is my joy. He likes to listen to *fiabe*" (fairy tales), she told me proudly.

More than once in the late afternoon, I saw Fabrizio sitting on Teresa's lap, enthralled with tales of primeval forests and enchanted castles.

"*C'era una volta . . .*" (Once upon a time), Teresa always began.

Teresa liked to talk, and when she spoke within the context of my limited Italian, especially to Fabrizio, she played with words. Sometimes during these storytelling hours, I heard howling winds, crashing thunder, and baying dogs. I heard exaggerations that oozed like molasses from her lips. *Aaatrocità! Solidaaarietà! Faaavoloso!* Embellishments pranced like ponies through her language. "*Mollllto! Grannnnde! Millllle!*"

Always I saw a bright-eyed little boy absorbed in the moment.

And just as I had taken an interest in her family, Teresa took an interest in mine. Whenever Marianna cleaned my room, and Teresa sometimes helped her, I could hear them say, "*Un bell'uomo!*" (handsome man) as they studied John's picture in the silver frame.

"Alzheimer's. *Terribile,*" they commiserated, shaking their heads with the same dismay, as if this malaise had settled into their own families.

*L*ife in Teresa's *pensione* was life reduced to simple terms, and I liked that. Life without complexities after years of complications—the numbing diagnosis, the descent into hopelessness, my depression, and then even the stressful Bertucci complications. In Teresa's *pensione,* my room had no radio, television, or phone, and its bathroom was down the hall. What it had in spades, however, was heart, and that's what I wanted.

*F*ather Pietro, the gentle priest who had brought me to Teresa's, was a small, blue-eyed man in his mid-fifties with a huge shock of gray hair. His mother died when he was a baby and his father couldn't cope with raising a child. He was brought up in an orphanage. Once when I asked Pietro why he had become a priest, he replied, "Only God would have me."

The moment Pietro steps into a room, the walls seem to burst with light. He owns hardly anything—a bicycle, shorts, a few T-shirts, sandals, a windbreaker, and his clerical gear.

A painter by training, his art graces walls around the globe. As a member of the university's art faculty, he lectures brilliantly on such topics as "scientific perspective," readily illustrating his talks with walking tours to Masaccio's Holy Trinity (located in Santa Maria Novella, a church built by the Dominicans from 1279 to 1357).

In his adjunct role as dean of students, Father Pietro ministered to his flock like a loving nanny, lending money when he had no money to lend and surreptitiously providing meals for those who were hard pressed to provide them for themselves. Sickbeds were his bailiwick; nightclubs, which his charges liked to frequent, his beat. A star marathoner, he routinely finished two-digit Ks all over Italy. At Christmas he took the students to the Holy Lands; in the winter, to the shrine of the Mother of Medjugorje in Bosnia; in the spring, after final exams, to Kenya and Mt. Kilimanjaro.

Long ago Pietro forgave his father for relinquishing him as a little boy; in fact, he now visits him in northern Italy several times a year.

While he had a good handle on most things, in some matters, Pietro was a bit impractical. One day as Frazer and I walked with him along Via de' Tornabuoni, en route to his art studio on Via

Palazzuolo, Pietro said, "My toilet's not working. There must be something wrong with the electricity."

"Your toilet works on electricity?" I asked quizzically.

Frazer rolled his eyes, then winked at me, and said tactfully, "Well, maybe in Italy toilets work on electricity."

Later that afternoon, Frazer checked Pietro's toilet. It operated from a water tank like toilets around the world. Frazer fixed it easily.

Adorable Father Pietro. A boy-man with such exquisite innocence, but also with a disarming sense of humor. Nonjudgmental and totally forgiving, he was someone with whom one could discuss anything.

On a brisk and sunny November day, we were in his art studio, an off-campus, hole-in-the-wall commercial space with a two-burner hot plate for impromptu pasta luncheons. A fresco class had just ended. Most of the students had departed. I was helping him clean up.

In jest I said to Pietro, "If you weren't a priest, I could run off with you."

Father Pietro giggled and blushed and said, "Well, I am, so don't get any ideas."

"Okay," I said with feigned sadness. After a pause, I added, "But I just have to ask, Have you ever loved a woman?"

"Yes, I have, and if you're asking 'Are you a virgin?', I'm not."

Startled by his directness, I replied, "That's good."

"Why?" he asked.

"So you can imagine how much I miss John," I replied.

"I can, Rose Marie, I can. I lost someone too," he said as he lifted a container of fresco plaster onto a shelf. "I was in my thirties when I was ordained. Prior to that there had been a woman . . ."

"What happened to her?"

"She married someone else," Pietro said with what seemed a hint of sadness.

"Did that hurt a lot?"

"At the time it did, but after a while I got over it. It was my faith in God, my belief that maybe there was another calling for me, and there was. I am at peace with my decision to become a priest."

My eyes flickered over the simple crucifix that hung around his neck.

"Any regrets?"

"Not really. There might have been moments when I wished I had had children. But when I was young, it seemed that people in my life were always coming and going, but God was a pretty sure thing."

"And He's always been there for you?"

"Yes, God is home base. I like hanging out in His neighborhood."

"Has God ever let you down?" I asked as my thoughts turned to John and a feeling of abandonment swept over me.

Father Pietro sensed this. He put his hand on my shoulder.

"Not really. I haven't always gotten what I've prayed for, but in the end what I have gotten was just right for me. God manifests in many guises."

CHAPTER 13

A Visit to a
Stud Farm

"Everything that lives, even a common domestic housefly,
has something of value to share with you—whenever you
are ready for the experience."
—J. ALLEN BOONE,
The Language of Silence

About a month after I moved into Teresa's under-maintained *pen-sione*, broken pipes flooded four rooms, mine included. Those of us affected by the deluge had to evacuate for ten days while repairs were made. I rented a room at Hotel Alpi, one of the two Florence hotels in which the American university housed its students. When friends asked why I didn't live with the students in the first place, my answer was simple: "Their lifestyle is too frenetic, their energy too boundless."

"They don't even start going to their discos until ten o'clock at night and sometimes don't come home until well after midnight," Frazer told me. He also lived apart. Besides, I just liked the warm familial mood of Teresa's. I needed to heal and I could in her nurturing environment.

An easy ten-minute walk to the palazzo, Hotel Alpi was owned and operated by a radiant young couple in their thirties whom Father Martini had married years before—Paolo and Marcella.

Paolo was a future Teresa—a land baron in the making. In 1995 he owned only Hotel Alpi, which he managed himself, even doing the cooking, but it was clear that he'd soon build upon his success. Paolo came from Italy's deep south, Calabria. His skin was bronze, his hair black, his teeth perfect and pearl white. "A gorgeous hunk," one of the girl students said when he wasn't around. He was gregarious and could laugh a blue streak even about Italy's notorious inefficiencies.

Marcella was lithe and golden blond, or, as Frazer said more than once, "She's easy on the eyes." In contrast to Teresa, a generation older, Marcella had conquered technology. She could make a computer sing and dance. And I thought Marcella had eyes in the back of her head. Few student antics slipped by her. Not even a supposedly hidden lovers' hideaway at the top of an elevator shaft.

Although Paolo and Marcella were childless, they had an adoring family—two almost human dogs, Lucietta, a fluffy Lhasa Apso, and Falstaff, a rescued and eternally grateful Great Dane.

Since I was "a mature student" and in the noncredit program, which meant there was no conflict of interest, adminstrators and faculty sometimes invited me to join them in their social activities. Shortly after the start of fall semester, Paola and Marcella invited Father Martini and several other university people to a trout grill at their home in the rolling green hills above Florence. Father Martini kindly invited me to join the group.

A brilliant day. Pure air and everywhere I looked I saw silhouettes of tall cypress trees. Vines draped the distant hills, the grape leaves not yet beginning to show autumn colors.

As we drove through this Tuscan splendor, the narrow road eventually led us to an iron gate and from there to a wonderful gray stone house—solidly built, seasoned, and lovingly tended. A stream burbled through the front yard and two dogs romped in high-spirited abandon.

The moment we stepped from our car, I heard a joyous cacophony of *buon giornos, piaceres, come stas, molto benes*. After the social amenities were over, Paolo directed our attention to Lucietta and Falstaff, who seemed busy sizing up soft touches, nudging those they deemed potential food droppers, and frolicking about like two indulged children.

1 am an animal lover. Twice in my life I have had the joy of owning collies. Champ was the last. He died shortly before John came into my life. While John and I courted, I sometimes felt that he might even be jealous of my long-dead dog.

After our marriage, I suggested to John that we get a dog. I knew that he liked them. For years, he had owned a dachshund, Carney, inherited from his first marriage. John and Carney were pals. When John left the house each morning to go to work, his parting words to Carney were, "You're in charge."

"Carney took these words very seriously," John told me once with a chuckle. "The torch was being passed. His watch was beginning. When I came home after work, he gladly surrendered his watch. It was like 'Whew! A long shift.' On weekends when I worked in the yard, he worked right beside me, digging in the dirt, jumping in the leaves, usually making a bigger mess than I wanted. We were part-ners, Carney and I. Buddies. I hated to see him die."

So it surprised me when John hemmed and hawed about getting a dog shortly after our marriage. Finally, one day, as I pressed for a decision, he confessed: "I don't want a dog because I don't want a rival."

With that, I decided to table the subject, to settle into our new marriage first and revisit the dog issue later. But then John got sick.

Since my room at Hotel Alpi was near the reception area, I quick-ly caught on to the hotel's routine. The sleepy-eyed night clerk, Taddeo, left at 7 a.m. each weekday morning when Paolo and Marcella arrived at work. And they always arrived with Lucietta in busy attendance.

Lucietta was small. She could be lifted, moved, and tucked here and there as needs arose. She had a busy schedule. For one thing, immediately upon arriving, she had to greet between forty and fifty of the adoring students. She had to endure being cuddled, cradled, and stroked. Some girl students insisted that her profuse, sand-col-ored, long coat be combed. To her complete dismay, one student even suggested to Marcella that she be bathed. But these were minor vexations. Her real concern was supervising the guests' comings and goings, especially the students who all seemed to have different schedules. She could hardly keep up. At mealtime, she had to posi-tion herself just right for perfect food droppings. Not everyone in the hotel cared to give her tidbits. She had to cultivate her benefactors. And, because Hotel Alpi reserved a number of rooms for the general public, she had to take note of these other, nonstudent guests who came and went during the course of a week.

On the whole the hotel's clientele was good. Most of the nonstudent guests were travel-weary tourists who happily collapsed into their rooms at night. In contrast to the university students who stayed seven months, these nonstudent guests stayed a few nights, rarely more than a week. Still, it was Lucietta's job to keep track of everything.

Lucietta was friendly with me, but prudently so. She had more seasoned relationships to tend to first—longer-term relationships. Quite naturally, there was a pecking order and as a relative newcomer in her life, I was simply not yet on her "A list."

During my stay there, a priest arrived from Rome. I happened to be in the lobby when he approached the registration desk. A diminutive man with thick horn-rimmed glasses in an immaculate black clerical suit with Roman collar, he announced to Paolo in a soft-spoken voice that he had come to Florence to see the bishop. Just then Lucietta bustled into the reception area. The minute she saw the priest from Rome, she stopped dead in her tracks. Her eyes latched onto the man with X-ray vision. Then she growled and growled again. Paolo, a good Catholic and embarrassed at his dog's seeming disrespect for a man of the cloth, said, "Lucietta, BASTA! VAI VIA!" (Stop it! Go away!)

Lucietta recoiled at the sound of those words. Clearly, "BASTA! VAI VIA!" were loathsome words to her, undeserved words, wounding words, for one who worked so hard. Still, she was an obedient dog and crept away under a heavy wooden chair where Paolo could not see her, but with her brown oval eyes she could observe everything. After the priest and Paolo exchanged pleasant words, the man went to his room.

Feeling sorry for her, I called playfully, "Lucietta, come!" Lucietta crawled out from under her chair and in the midst of good fun forgot about the priest from Rome.

On the next day when the priest came to the antique-filled dining room for breakfast, she again reacted the same way. Again, she growled. Again, Paolo said, "*BASTA! VAI VIA!*"

Before she could hide from Paolo's jarring words, she heard the coveted, "Lucietta, come!" The students were heading off to class. Some wanted one last cuddle. Soon she was engulfed in adulation while the priest said something to Paolo about meeting with the monsignor that day.

The priest stayed for six days. Each day he spoke of his important appointments. On the seventh day, late in the afternoon, the priest said to Paolo, "You know, I meant to cash a check at the bank today, but just didn't get to it and now the banks are closed until tomorrow morning."

"I can cash a check for you," Paolo replied, more than ready to help a priest. "How much would you like?"

The priest said the equivalent of $800.00.

Paolo gave him the cash. The priest left on an errand and never returned.

On the next day, when Paolo came back from the bank, he told me, "The priest's check bounced."

The police came. "We're on to this impostor who moves from hotel to hotel professing to be a priest and cashing bogus checks."

Paolo patted Lucietta saying, "You had it figured out right from the start, didn't you, girl?"

After that Paolo vowed to run every check that passed through his establishment by Lucietta. If she growled, it meant trouble.

*F*or some time Paolo and Marcella had mentioned that perhaps one day Falstaff should be bred.

"He's such a magnificent specimen," Paolo liked to say with paternal pride. "We don't know his exact age. It would be nice to have his son."

Because Falstaff was nearly the size of a small pony, he had to spend workdays at home alone waiting for his family's afternoon return within the confines of the large fenced yard.

From my visit to Falstaff's home, I gathered that his days there were mainly days of rest, occasionally diverted by rabbits that scampered across his lawn or neighbor cats that jumped his fence. Sometimes ducks and geese refreshed themselves along his stream, but generally his routine was peaceful. Usually he lazed away the hours, maybe contemplating his good fortune to have been rescued by such lovable people as Paolo and Marcella from the cellar in which his previous owner had chained him.

"In that cellar he never saw the sun," Falstaff's defender, Paolo, told me with indignation. "There he never saw the sky. Never a rabbit. Never a cat. Never had enough to eat. Now with us and our hotel that serves three square meals a day, the leftovers must be to die for."

One day during my stay at the Hotel Alpi, Paolo said, "I know a farmer, Cosimo, near Arezzo. His female Great Dane will soon be in heat. We've decided that at the appropriate time our dogs will be mated."

Soon it was time. On a Saturday morning, Paolo coaxed Falstaff into the back of his *quattro ruote* (four-wheel vehicle). Marcella was tagging along and asked me to join them. I had never been to Arezzo before. I only knew that it had one of the biggest gold jewelry industries in Europe, that it was a center for antiques, and that Petrarch had been born there.

We tore along country roads, eventually sliding onto a motorway heading south. After what must have seemed like an interminable amount of time to Falstaff, who appeared to lie miserably crunched in the back of the *quattro ruote*, we arrived at a farm with a stone house not dissimilar from his own. A man came out.

"*Buon giorno*, Cosimo," Paolo said buoyantly.

"*Buon giorno*, Paolo," the man replied with equal enthusiasm. "*Buon giorno, signora*," he said nodding at both Marcella and me simultaneously.

Cosimo and Paolo chatted. The man took a long, hard look into the backseat as if to evaluate Falstaff, who, under Paolo's adoring care, had blossomed into a healthy specimen. Cosimo nodded approvingly. Then Paolo stepped out of the vehicle and opened the back door. Falstaff bounded into freedom.

After several minutes of conversation, the two men lured Falstaff into a fenced courtyard. There Falstaff encountered a beautiful fawn-colored dog very much like himself. It was love at first sight. Gina, too, seemed enamored of the gentle giant who stood before her.

The two dogs gamboled and danced.

Time evaporated.

The owners waited for nature to take its course. But nothing happened. Falstaff didn't know what to do. The owners cajoled and prodded and even acted out various possibilities, but Falstaff only stood dumbfounded at the strange antics of the two men.

As for Marcella and me, we laughed so hard that tears rolled down our cheeks.

After continued play between the two dogs, but without copulation, Paolo and Cosimo decided to try again on another day with the help of a vet.

On the way home we stopped briefly in Arezzo to check out its famous antiques fair. Marcella collected old furniture, but knowing that they had an uncomfortable Falstaff in the back of the car, they decided to forgo their furniture hunt and drive back to their house in the Florence hills.

On the appointed day, Paolo once again coaxed Falstaff into the *quattro ruote* and once again, Marcella and I again came along for the ride. This time Falstaff and Gina were joined by the vet, Dr. Bencini. Falstaff took no notice of the vet; he had eyes only for Gina.

Again, the two dogs gamboled. Again, Paolo and Cosimo cajoled. Again, Falstaff stood as if amazed at the buffoonishness of the two men.

Then Dr. Bencini stepped in. When nothing else seemed to work, the vet literally mounted Falstaff over Gina.

Falstaff thought it was a game.

Finally, in desperation, Dr. Bencini himself mounted Falstaff, who was mounted on Gina, and with a series of swift thrusting motions gave him a clue on what to do.

After an appropriate interval, Gina delivered several puppies; the one named Carlo went to live with Paolo and Marcella.

*A*fter my room in Teresa's *pensione* had been repaired, I moved back to my old space. Repairing the pipe damage had taken a full three weeks, not a mere ten days. Still, I liked my room with all its imperfections—the creaking bed, the cracked marble floor, the tattered curtains, the stopped-up sink. And I liked Teresa's warm way.

"*Come mi fa piacere rivederti, Rosa,*" (How happy it makes me to see you again) Teresa said when I checked back in.

"*Grazie mille,*" I answered. "I have much to tell you," I added as I thought about the impostor priest and Falstaff and Gina.

"We will talk soon," Teresa said as she answered the piercing telephone ring.

I visited Hotel Alpi often. When I ate there and Marcella wasn't looking, I fed Lucietta small tidbits from the table—an act that soon elevated me to Lucietta's A list.

CHAPTER 14

Shared Atrocities

> "We cannot lose once we realize that everything that happens
> to us has been designed to teach us holiness."
> —DONALD NICHOLL, *Holiness*

One evening, not long after I had moved back into her *pensione,* as Teresa sat alone mending curtains in the reception area that doubled as her living room, she motioned me to join her. (Salvatore was at the other *pensione* making repairs.) She was drinking chamomile tea and offered me a cup. After recounting my experiences at Hotel Alpi, Teresa, ever one to like a good story, asked, "What is it like where you are from?"

"The northwestern United States is rugged, mountainous, with lots of lakes and rivers, much like Bavaria in Germany where I was born," I replied.

Teresa's facial muscles tightened. She looked at me carefully and said, "I thought you were an American."

"I am, but a naturalized one. I came to the States as a college student, married, and just stayed on."

Always direct, Teresa then said, "The Nazis made me learn German as a child. I don't like the German language, but it's now useful with my German-speaking guests."

Aware that she might have shown too much of an edge, Teresa went on, "I understand that not every German during the war was a Nazi, and those who pass through my *pensione* today are hardly responsible for the war." *But still, they're the offspring of a people who could bring about such cruelty.* I could hear the underlying message in her tone.

Remembering the Nazi history in Italy during World War II, I realized that I had struck a sensitive chord. More than once in my life, I had met a suspicion of things German, as if there might be some collective evil ingrained in the descendants of the people who had allowed the Third Reich to come into being.

Nationalistic pride within the countries of the European Union continues to loom large. Italians still like being Italians, the British, British, and the French, French. For Teresa and Salvatore's generation, the foreign invasions of Italy brought on by World War II were too cataclysmic ever to be fully erased.

While the war was a delicate subject that touched old wounds, it eventually bonded us. We were both products of that era. We were both children then, war victims. Teresa was born in 1933, I in 1940. Over the months of our friendship, we occasionally shared war stories in the evening over a beverage.

Teresa listened as much as she talked.

During one of our evening conversations, she asked, "Did your family know about the atrocities that occurred in Germany during the war years?"

"Not a clue until 1943," I told her. "We were ordinary citizens. Male members of my family were conscripted. But in 1943 something awful happened.

"My mother had a cousin, Florian, in his late teens who had been drafted into Hitler's army early in the war and sent to a mysterious destination about which he could never speak. On furloughs home to his family's small farm near Bamberg, he always showed uncharacteristic signs of stress, and even depression. He clearly hated what he was doing, but he could never talk about it. The last day at home was always a wrench.

"While on leave in 1943 he was more depressed than ever. He spent hours looking off into space. His mother, Gertrud, was worried, but what could she do? Notify the military? Talk to his superior?

Depression during war is common. They give crybabies short shrift. Besides, the Nazis need everything that walks. They're recruiting males from age fifteen to sixty. A little depression, forget it.

"At one point during the visit, Helmut told his mother, 'I'm going to take a bath.'

"Gertrud didn't think much about that—only that a bath might do him good.

"The bath water ran. Time passed. The clock ticked. After a while, Gertrud began to wonder why he would be in the tub so long. She knocked on the door. There was no answer. *Maybe he fell asleep.* She got another member of the family and together they banged on the door and rattled the doorknob. No answer. Finally, they knocked down the bathroom door. In the tub they found Florian with his wrists slit, dead.

"Later the family learned that his assignment had been at a Nazi death camp. Suicide was better than returning to that."

Teresa sat solemnly for a moment as if to absorb the impact of the story.

"Until now I have not thought much about ordinary German citizens who were also put in harm's way by the Nazi regime," she admitted quietly.

Needing a break after this sobering tale, Teresa rose from her chair asking, *"Ancora un po' di tè?"* (More tea?)

"*Sì*, I'll take another cup. *Grazie*."

When she returned with the tea, Teresa sat thoughtfully, as if she were mulling over wartime memories of her own.

"The war was a difficult time for me," she said softly. "I spent months in an orphanage, and because I was older, I helped look after younger children. After the war I was reunited with my family in Livorno, but many children were not that lucky."

Just as Teresa was about to continue with her account of the war, Salvatore shambled into the lobby announcing proudly, "*Ho riparato il lavandino!*" (I fixed the sink!) He then bent over to kiss Teresa's cheek saying, "*Bellezza mia.*" (My beauty)

"*Bravo, tesoro* (treasure)," Teresa answered warmly.

Salvatore wandered into the kitchen to collect his inevitable red wine, and exhausted from the day's activity, plopped down beside Teresa. He reached for his glass and drank deeply.

Salvatore was eighty years old and disheveled. His trousers hung from his body only by the grace of suspenders. On some days he forgot to shave. Sometimes a shoelace flopped untied. His fingernails usually needed trimming. But he didn't care about these minor details. What he did care about was helping Teresa run the family business. The family mattered, and God mattered.

The demands of the *pensioni* were clearly too much for him. But he, like Teresa, knew no other life.

"They could easily retire," Father Pietro told me, "but to quit would be to die. This way they're in the stream of life. The world comes to them."

On this evening Salvatore wanted to talk about wine, and Teresa, mellow from the evening's easy pace, readily surrendered the stage.

"This is *our* wine," Salvatore said proudly as he raised his glass against the light to savor the liquid's deep red glow. "It comes from *Chianti Classico* which is the best producing area in Italy. Since Chianti wines come from a whole region, the name Chianti is no guarantee of goodness," Salvatore discoursed, well pleased with his fount of knowledge.

"As with most things, you have to know the winemaker and the precise location of the vineyard. Labels can be misleading," he added.

As an afterthought, he said, "*We* have a good location."

Salvatore liked the stage, but Teresa rarely let him have it; wine, however, was his specialty and on that subject Teresa acquiesced and listened patiently.

After more sips and even more detailed information about oak barrels, the hills of the Chianti region, the *consorzio* of producers in that region and their standards, Teresa interrupted our conversation: "Ah, here comes Gaspare."

In came the nightclerk, a straw-haired young man laden with books. It was ten o'clock.

"*Buona sera,*" he said politely.

"*Buona sera,*" we said simultaneously.

A student at the University of Florence, Gaspare came each evening from ten until one when the *pensione* closed for the night. A few guests straggled in during his shift, but usually it was quiet and he could study. Woe to those who arrived after one in the morning. Teresa's lock-out policy was merciless.

After several rounds of *buona notte,* Teresa, Salvatore, and I retired to our respective rooms.

My fourth-floor room looked out over a sea of contiguous red-tiled roofs. Sometimes at night I fancied that I could walk across much of Florence just by stepping out of my window and tiptoeing like a cat burglar across the shaded peaks and valleys that lay before me. (In fact, I met a woman whose lover lived two rooftops away.

Under the cover of darkness, they sometimes traveled to each other's apartments via their adjoining roofs. A nosy neighbor, thinking that the shadowy figures were burglars, called the police, who put an end to these rooftop trysts.)

Salvatore had gotten me a reading lamp to keep by my bed. At night it cast a cozy glow around my room, softening the effect of the beat-up furniture, the stone floor, and white walls with their shadows of light and dark. This cubicle was so much simpler than the house I had shared with John, and yet it gradually replaced those ornate rooms of death in my mind's eye. This tiny, freeing space was my launchpad to a new life.

For the time being it was my home where I could bury myself under blankets and read until all hours. But some nights I couldn't fall asleep and I didn't want to read. I wanted simply to lie there thinking about all that had happened during the past year. Day by day my time in Florence seemed to squeeze out the convulsive experience of John's death.

CHAPTER 15

Heroes Bringing Gifts of Light

"A hero ventures forth from the world of common day
into a region of supernatural wonder: fabulous forces
are there encountered and a decisive victory is won:
the hero comes back from this mysterious adventure with
the power to bestow boons on his fellow man."
—JOSEPH CAMPBELL,
The Hero with a Thousand Faces

Professor Eric Petersen taught a course called Excursions in Philosophy. An American, married to a Tuscan, he lived on a small farm not far from Siena and commuted to Florence to teach us.

One day, while discussing myths, Professor Petersen mentioned the classical hero who typically goes into great darkness where he battles evil on many fronts, returning eventually with "light" for the world he left behind. He added, "We're all potential heroes because we all go into dark places. The question is, what do we bring back?"

It hit me forcefully that I had just emerged from a very dark place. Was there something I could bring back? To whom? It was too soon.

He assigned each of us to write a paper on a darkness we had traveled through and to comment on what we brought back to our community from that experience.

"Oh, shit," a student named Doug grumbled when he heard the assignment. We all knew Doug was in this class to get what he thought would be an easy A. "It's all bullshit," he said about nearly everything.

Doug's parents had met in this Florence program twenty-five years earlier. He had been coded since birth to undertake this study-abroad adventure. A reluctant student, but a good one when he applied himself, his most pressing problem was substance abuse. He was a "potter."

I couldn't bring myself to write about John yet. So instead I wrote my paper about a childhood incident in which we were miraculously saved by an act of compassion. Not only was I here today because of it, but it had guided my entire life, including those ordeal years with John.

Although born in Munich in 1940, I spent my early years in Würzburg, a town about three hours north by train. I can't remember having a childhood in the normal sense of the word. I can't remember toys or, for that matter, much play. What I remember mainly are stories—great, wonderful stories told to me on my grandfather's lap where unassuming heroes crushed enemies, won king-doms, and married princesses.

It was only later that I realized that these hours, cradled in the safety of my grandfather's storytelling embrace, had in some small way created my sense of how life should flow. I think that my time with my grandfather influenced my early thinking about love, com-passion, generosity, and strength and lay the foundation for my later care of John.

On March 16, 1945, as the Allies prepared for Germany's final surrender, Würzburg suffered an unexpected and devastating nighttime aerial attack. But my family was lucky. While nearly all the buildings around us were hit by explosive bombs, the one that hit our building was an incendiary bomb. That bought us time. While the upper stories of the structure in which we had enjoyed a second-floor apartment roared in flames, we managed to escape through basement windows. Out of doors, the earth around us reverberated with explosions, the sky blazed orange. Gusts of heat assaulted us. The smell of burning flesh choked us as we raced, stumbled, to an underground bunker where horror-filled screams of dying soldiers and civilians filled the night air. I hud-dled in my only clothing—a thin nightgown and one pink-flow-ered slipper—near the entrance on one of the benches that ringed the inside of the bunker. From there we heard the last of the British bombers drone west and we watched our home burn to the ground.

We were now refugees. We had lost everything except the clothes on our backs. But even as a child of not quite five, I sensed my family's elation that we had escaped the devastation unhurt. Not one member of my extended family had been killed in the air raid, although it had destroyed eighty percent of our town.

"Danke dass Du uns behuettest hast," (Thank you, God, for

protecting us), my deeply religious grandmother prayed while the rest of us gave thanks in our own personal ways.

Within a few days, we were evacuated to the village of Waldturm, some kilometers south of Würzburg. And it is the gypsy who helped us relocate who still fascinates me.

My grandfather was a banker. He made loans. In 1943, two years before the Allied victory over Europe, a gypsy named Alexa had come to him asking for money. I never knew how it was that Alexa and his family had been spared the Nazi policy of extermination, but I surmise that because he was not migratory, had a permanent residence, and pursued a regular occupation, he was left alone.

At any rate, my grandfather took a liking to Alexa and lent him the money. Within the next two years, Alexa repaid the loan to the penny and he and my grandfather stayed in touch.

Inexplicably, two days after the bombing, as Würzburg lay in ruin, Alexa found us in the bunker and said to my grandfather, "You helped me in my time of need. Maybe now I can help you. There's a village to the south, Waldturm, that still has room for a few more refugees. I can take you and your family there in my horse cart."

Desperate and with no other choices, my grandfather gratefully accepted the offer.

Within a day or two, my grandparents, an aunt with a newborn baby, my mother, and I piled into Alexa's cart.

The road to Waldturm moseyed easily through forested farmland.

We had just spent days living by our wits with no real shelter except the bunker that we shared with the wounded. After days of terror, we believed that this four-hour journey on back-country roads would be a time of repose—an opportunity to collect ourselves.

For a while we were right.

But it was only March 20, 1945, almost two months before Germany's unconditional surrender on May 8, and the war still raged.

Two hours into the trip, suddenly from nowhere, two low-flying

American fighter planes spotted us and at treetop level began to strafe our little band of refugees.

We dove into roadside bushes.

Frozen in fear, we lay on the ground, clutching shrubbery, trees, logs—anything that might bring stability amidst the pandemonium surrounding us.

We prayed out loud to God.

Miraculously, not one bullet hit us.

When we thought the fighters were gone, we climbed back into our cart. Just then the planes circled back for a second run. Again we dove into bushes. More bullets poured over us.

Why? I remember my family asking. *We are simple civilians, a fact that is clearly visible from treetop level. Three older people. A young mother with her newborn baby. Another young mother with a four-year-old girl. Why are they attacking us?*

Again we prayed. Again, not one bullet hit us.

This time we waited many minutes before venturing forth again. Motionless, nearly afraid to breathe, we cowered in the bushes.

"Let them think they've finished us off," Alexa cautioned us.

When he felt certain that the Americans had given up, Alexa said, *"Wir machen weiter."* (We'll continue.)

With that, our little caravan rolled on, arriving in Waldturm before nightfall.

Within minutes of reaching the village, Alexa, who had appeared so mysteriously when we needed him and ferried us so tenderly, said warm good-byes to each of us.

We never saw him again.

As an adult I have often driven the route we traveled with Alexa that day. At times, I've stopped at the precise spot where the bullets sprayed us.

Does the ground there still hold those bullets? If I dug in the dirt, would I find them?

During our first days in Waldturm, we slept on straw. Eventually we were allotted two simple rooms in a farmhouse—our home for the next three years.

May 8, 1945, the official date of Germany's surrender, was still weeks away. For now, the U.S. Army in full battle gear tanked across what would be the U.S. Zone. Most towns and villages capitulated readily, but a few, Waldturm included, resisted occupation. Bullets scorched the air. Bombs dropped. We hid in cellars. We concealed ourselves in barns. In the midst of all the confusion, a young playmate my age, Rolf, a fellow refugee too young to understand the politics of war, was shot and killed. His father was missing in the war, his mother beyond consolation. It was my first encounter with death.

Devastated that Rolf could no longer play with me, I remember wondering where he would go. Into a coffin and into the ground, yes, but adults around me kept saying he would go to heaven to be with the angels. I remember wondering where that place was.

I viewed Rolf in his coffin just before burial. His mother stood bereaved, weeping over her child. The boy looked angelic, decked out in white. I could not believe he was dead. He looked more like he was resting or playing possum, like we used to when he was alive. His eyes were still open. I thought that if I tapped him on the shoulder he would wake up. We could play make-believe again. I remembered how at that moment, with a reverence that only a mother can convey, Rolf's mother reached down to her son's eyes and closed them. She was sobbing. Instinctively, I knew that this gesture bespoke a dreadful finality. Her son was gone. My friend would never chase me through the springtime meadows again. In absolute horror I fled from the room determined to have as little to do with death as possible.

Somehow Rolf was buried in the turmoil of the next few days, during which the German holdouts were killed or arrested and our village surrendered and became officially occupied by the U.S. Army.

Oddly, our salvation during these extraordinary times was the United States Army.

Within a few days of Waldturm's surrender, the U.S. Army decided that we—now a sorry lot of women, children, and a few old men—were harmless. They became our friends, giving us chocolate bars, oranges, and bananas. Because of wartime rationing, I and the other young children of the village had never seen or tasted such delicacies before.

Some soldiers took us for rides in their jeeps. Some played ball with us. Some showed us pictures of their wives and children. One soldier, seeing that I had no shoes, brought me a new pair.

Since my mother could speak some English, the U.S. Army hired her as an interpreter. Seeing our poverty, a few soldiers broke military law by slipping my mother coffee and cigarettes to use in bartering for food on the black market. These gestures, although illegal, were godsends. Occasionally, when my grandmother was lucky enough to have a few illegal cigarettes at her disposal, she would take me by the hand, and march me from farmhouse to farmhouse, telling whoever answered the door, "I will give you two cigarettes for one fresh egg to feed this child."

I believe that these experiences helped lay the foundation for my lifelong optimism, an attitude that I could convey to John even during his ordeal. Yes, bad things happen to us, but a lot of good things too. And maybe the "bad" is not so much bad as an important lesson. Nothing is ever lost. "All happenings form a unity," Plotinus said. This attitude was to stand me in good stead during my own struggle with John. And later, my wartime childhood formed the bedrock of my struggle to heal.

CHAPTER 16

The Mafia and Art

"We become brave by doing brave acts."
—ARISTOTLE, *Nicomachean Ethics*

$\mathcal{A}$s the weeks passed I occasionally ran into Professor Raffanelli at a nearby *bar* that served delicious ready-made luncheon sandwiches. When alone, she often asked me to join her. We were nearly the same age and we shared the heritage of switching continents of birth. She was an American who had married into Europe; I was a European who had married into the United States. And, as mentioned earlier, in her classes I was an auditor, not a credit-seeking student; hence, conflict-of-interest pressures between us were off. We could be friends and, indeed, we were.

Graceful and elegant, Professor Raffanelli, had met and married a Florentine in the 1960s while a postgraduate student in art history.

For a quarter of a century now she and her husband had lived on a Tuscan farm where they produced wine and olive oil. Three days a week she bused into Florence to lecture at our university. She never had children, but says generously, "I have 5,000 children." They are her students—those she has taught over nearly three decades. Many still correspond with her. I do. She is a gracious, patrician lady with whom you could not pick a fight. But she does insist on excellence.

The *bar* in which we met was nondescript, perhaps the size of an American home garage with a loft of five or six small round tables. Its attraction was its proximity to the university. "Twenty paces," Giorgio, our palazzo's friendly concierge, liked to say when he directed thirsty tourists in its direction.

During one luncheon occasion, as we shared small talk, Professor Raffanelli directed my glance to a swarthy looking man just getting up from his table and moving toward the exit.

"Mafia," she whispered and then, as if wanting to defuse the impact of what she had just said, added delicately, "So it's rumored."

I saw a man with curly dark hair, bull-necked and stoutly built, but small. As he moved across the loft, he nodded to another patron in the *bar.* I sensed a belligerency about him, a man of set purpose who was used to getting what he wanted.

Once he was out of the *bar,* I asked, "Is there much evidence of the Mafia around here?"

"It exists," she answered as she bit into her *panino* that dripped with mozzarella and sweet prosciutto.

"Does it affect the ordinary person's life? Has it affected your life?" I asked wanting to understand Italian society better.

She sat quietly for a moment as if to weigh the pros and cons of opening a Pandora's box. Then she said quietly, "Yes. It's touched my personal and professional life."

"In what way?" I asked.

She looked at her watch and said "Do you have time for an espresso?"

*I*t seems that some years before, Professor Raffanelli had in her art history class a student she called Robert Molinari. According to reliable sources, Robert was the son of a big-time Mafia boss back in the States. The boy did everything but study. While most of the students scraped by on Eurail passes, he with his unlimited funds flew to all the travel destinations—Paris, London, Athens. He partied all night every night, often dragging into class the next morning smelling of stale alcohol. He failed more tests than he passed. She counseled him. Father Martini counseled him. Eventually, he failed Professor Raffanelli's entire first semester.

"I F'd him," she said in a way that suggested she was a person of principle and could not be bought or even intimidated by a potential threat.

Students in the Florence program rarely flunk. Those who apply to the program are carefully screened. To qualify, they need a strong academic track record and Robert had one. But Europe offered too many distractions.

Professor Raffanelli said she had some mild concerns about giving a *padrone's* son an F. She knew about the Cosa Nostra and their penchant for retribution. She had heard about torture and slow death. She had even read *The Godfather.* In fact, she had had a Mafia-related incident in her own circle of friends just two years before the situation with Robert occurred.

The family friend, Vito, who worked in an Italian industrial city, had to fire two incompetent employees. Within a few days after the firing, as Vito drove home from work and paused briefly at a stoplight, a car pulled up beside him. The man in the passenger seat of the parallel car drew a pistol from his jacket and shot Vito in the chest. Fortunately, that day Vito had a pen in his shirt pocket. The bullet hit the pen and then rebounded into the dashboard of his car.

Vito knew instantly what was happening. He threw himself onto the passenger seat. At the same time another bullet hit the passenger door and then another. The would-be assassin sped off. Vito suffered only minor injuries, but someone had put a contract out on him. It was years before he dared to go anywhere without government-supplied body guards.

Within three weeks after giving Robert the F, Father Martini advised her that the *padrone*, Mr. Molinari, was on his way to Florence.

Santa Maria!

"I truly began to worry about my safety and my husband's safety as well," she said as we started sipping our espressos.

Mr. Molinari's arrival was even more bizarre than she had imagined. He came swishing into her 9:30 a.m. art history class in a brown full-length mink coat. A gold ring gleamed on his finger, a gold chain at his neck. Yet he had a genial face, framed by a receding hairline. He took a seat in the last row of the *Aula*, slumping casually and letting his mink spill across the terra-cotta floor with marble inlay. The students gaped at the stranger in the back row, but by now had seen enough of the exotic to be unfazed by the spectacle.

That day Professor Raffanelli lectured on sculpture during the early Renaissance, between 1400–1450, specifically on Donatello's *David* and *Mary Magdalen*.

Throughout, Mr. Molinari studied her carefully. In her agitated state, she thought each breath might be her last. Images of her blood spattered across the floor filled her mind. If it were her last act, she would teach her beloved art history well. Mr. Molinari actually appeared to be quite attentive, as if he might be tracking the lecture, but then, maybe he was just plotting her demise. Robert sat near his father, trying hard to pretend that he didn't know the man.

After class, as the other students filed out of the *Aula*, Mr. Molinari gathered up his voluminous mink coat, flung it across his shoulders and with determined steps walked up to her lectern. Robert followed him, but kept a safe distance.

"Good lecture, Professor," Mr. Molinari said in a soft-spoken voice.

"Thank you," she answered cautiously, unsure of what to expect next.

After one or two other social amenities, Mr. Molinari said, "I gotta hand it to you, Professor. You're the first person who's ever had the nerve to stand up to my boy. Thank you. As for the F and the bad study habits, we're gonna tackle those together. No son of mine is gonna settle for an F."

Robert looked stricken.

With that the two marched out of the *Aula* and into the administrative offices for a talk with Father Martini.

At the end of the second semester, Robert had earned an A in art history.

CHAPTER 17

A Myth for Teresa

"Some say that community is based on blood ties, sometimes
dictated by choice, sometimes by necessity. And while this
is quite true, the immeasurably stronger gravitational field
that holds a group together are their stories . . . the common
and simple ones they share with one another."
—CLARISSA PINKOLA ESTES,
The Gift of Story

*L*ater that day, while in the *pensione's* lobby checking train schedules to San Marino, I observed Teresa sitting at her desk reconciling
ledgers, and Salvatore hobbling on crutches. He had twisted his
ankle a few days before while he and a city worker examined the
sewer line leading into their building.

Like an invalid, Salvatore lowered himself delicately into one of
the lobby's easy chairs and, with the tone of a little boy who wants
his mother, called to Teresa, *"Vieni da me."* (Come to me.)

As Teresa put her now-reconciled ledger into a folder of other ledgers, Salvatore poured three cups of chamomile tea and said, "Rosa, you sit with us for a while, too."

"*Grazie*, Salvatore," I replied, happy to enjoy their warm company. Soon Teresa, in her bedroom slippers, shuffled over to us and sank into soft upholstery. She took Salvatore's hand and meshed her fingers through his. Their eyes met. They smiled.

I half dreamed that John and I once sat like this, although, of course, we didn't. Not quite like this. We never meshed fingers; instead, he took my hand and put it in his lap and never let go. I was torn between joy in Teresa and Salvatore's love, and the awful realization once again that I was alone.

"*H*ow was your school day, Rosa?" Teresa asked.

"Oh, *benone, grazie,*" I said, still moved by Professor Raffanelli's Mafia story during lunch. Briefly, I outlined it and both Teresa and Salvatore smiled knowingly. I suspected they knew more about the Mafia than they let on.

"Let us talk about happy things," Teresa said diplomatically. Then abruptly my congenial inquisitor asked, "How did you and John meet?"

At first I was taken aback by her curiosity about my life, but Fiona, my Irish friend who had settled in Florence thirty years before, had told me, "Italians don't have the same sense of privacy that we Anglo-Saxons have." She said that, even today, what holds Italy together is not so much the *state* as the *family.* "In Italy, the concept of *family* includes far-flung cousins and even close friends." She added, "You've been adopted, Rose Marie, so get used to sharing family secrets."

So once again I began spilling my story, this time of John.

I began with our first meeting. I told them that I was blown away by his good looks and how jealous I felt later when I saw him with elegant matrons who could have been my mother. I told them how, a year after meeting him, I finally got up the nerve to ask him to attend a lecture with me, how he accepted and then reciprocated almost immediately, launching a wonderful three-year romance. I told them how John dragged his feet about proposing marriage and that it was only my family's visit to the United States that dislodged him from his comfortable single life.

Teresa and Salvatore smiled when I recalled how we'd fretted over the age-discrepancy thing and how Dr. Jackman reassured us that chronological age alone no longer necessarily decrees how we behave and live. Researchers who study aging now focus more on biological age, which looks at how well the body works, not how long it's been around.

I pictured for them John's old colonial house, buried in a tropical jungle, and his housekeeper, Sally, with her habit of borrowing other peoples belongings. I showed them my beautiful gold neck charm that reads *Ti amo più che mai*.

"*Ma che bello,*" Teresa said as she held it, reading the inscription and lifting its weight.

"John was a romantic?" Salvatore asked with a sparkle.

"*Sì,* in some ways, but also very practical, but he had his moments," I said nostalgically. Valentine's Day was his favorite holiday . . . tulips, daffodils, roses . . ."

After this small digression, I plunged into the first symptoms of Parkinson's and Alzheimer's.

Showing no signs of boredom, although I was now many minutes into my story, they nodded sympathetically when I described the subsequent chaos in our lives. I choked when I told them about John's courage, his agonizing cry to me one day, "I never do anything right,"—this from a man who had spent most of his life doing everything supremely well. I recounted my own turmoil, the vomiting and thoughts of my own impending death, and the saving grace of Dr. Reynolds.

As my story darkened, I waited for them to make some excuse to change the subject or leave. The hour was late and Salvatore wasn't feeling well. I couldn't believe that they would really want to hear about John's end, and, of course, I was shortening it considerably. Instead, Salvatore poured more tea, and even though Teresa's eyes were by now half-lidded with fatigue, he remained alert to my story, not just polite, but injecting an occasional comment of sympathy.

"*Dio mio*," Salvatore murmured when I told them of John's eventual surrender and how moments after he died a cluster of birds rested briefly in our yard.

"I've read that the ancient Romans believed that birds led human souls to heaven. Is that right?" I asked as I looked at both of them.

"*Sì, sì,*" Salvatore replied. "*Può darsi*" (It's possible), he added as he glanced at Teresa, seeking confirmation.

Teresa nodded and then began. "*Sì*, Rome believed in many gods, much like the Greeks."

"Pagan?" I asked.

"Yes. Before Christianity the Roman Empire teetered like a drunken man. They even believed in things like fate, chance, and astrology," the devoutly Catholic Teresa offered with dismay.

After a short pause during which Salvatore poured even more tea, he said pensively, "Your story about John reminds me of *La Bohème*."

"I hadn't thought of that," I answered, "but there is a connection in the sense that the two lovers in Puccini's opera, Mimi and Rodolfo, are torn apart by Mimi's untimely death. Lost love—a timeless tale."

I had told bits and pieces of my story to friends and relatives over and over again, but never the whole thing in one sitting from beginning to end. I was struck with the realization that it was indeed a *story* now, with a beginning, a middle, and an end, a *myth* to be handed down to others. It was my story and no one else could have the same one, although family members and caregivers might add their own twists and turns. As my myth, it was precious.

As Teresa and Salvatore listened, it struck me how differently they did so. I compared them to some of my acquaintances, people like Ginger and Connie, who wanted immediate solutions. They wanted to fix things. Put John in a nursing home. Plan a future for myself. Get on with my life. Get past this fast. Maybe then their own discomfort would go away. But Teresa and Salvatore just listened, completely accepting, sympathetic, as though it were an ancient tale. And in a way it was an ancient tale. As Northrop Frye writes in *The Educated Imagination,* "[The] story of the loss and regaining of identity is, I think, the framework of all literature."

I recalled how Dr. Reynolds had explained that part of the working-through-grief process was doing precisely what I had just done, telling my story, over and over again.

*B*efore our evening closed, Teresa told me a story about a woman who lived in a village where there was a shortage of men due to the war. More than anything, this woman wanted to marry and have a family. She wanted children, a house, animals, and eventually grandchildren. But it was not to be. Now she was in her seventies and still single. She had spent her life as a wonderful teacher to many children. She had a small house with animals, but the one experience she longed for most, being married, eluded her.

"But you had it, Rose Marie! Maybe not in the way you wanted, and not for long, but still, you had what this village woman never could. We don't always get what we want, and if we do, it's not always in the form we expect. For some, marriage is an end-of-the rainbow experience, for others a source of hell. God has his own agenda."

Spending this evening with Teresa and Salvatore took me a big step forward in my healing. It was an evening of acceptance and validation. Friendship, it reminded me, fortifies us. And it reinforced my feeling that I wouldn't have given up the entirety of my experience with John despite all the grieving that came afterward.

CHAPTER 18

Where Angels Tread

"Civilization is the long process of learning to be kind."
—ANONYMOUS

Most days in Florence were fast paced. Morning classes. Lunch. Afternoon classes. Homework. Cooking lessons. Evening classes. I started my study-abroad program with seven courses and soon dropped to five because I also wanted time to play.

Usually, on weekends, I went where the other students went— San Gimignano, Ravenna, Sicily, Cinque Terre. But when they camped, or wandered too far afield for my taste, I stayed at Teresa's to pursue more leisurely pleasures—a relaxed breakfast of bread, fruit, and *caffè latte*, a lazy read of *The International Tribune*, and an idle exchange with other guests in the *pensione*. There were lots of Germans. A few Swiss. Some Canadians. Occasional Americans.

Without fail, Teresa wandered through the breakfast area.

"*Buon giorno, Rosa. Come va?*"

"*Molto bene, grazie,*" I answered, emphasizing the *molto* because I now felt so content in my living situation.

"Where do you go today?"

"Cascine Park," I replied.

"*Oh, che meraviglia.*" (That's wonderful.)

After breakfast, I went back to my room, filled my backpack with reading material, a bottle of water and sunscreen, and then plodded off along Via dè Fossi toward the Arno and the park. Since it was by then October, the beech-and chestnut-filled hills around Florence had begun to blaze in seasonal colors of red and gold. Swifts performed aerial acrobatics high above me.

Early on along the banks of Tuscany's great watercourse, I had staked out a quiet place where I could recline against a stone wall that angled like an easy chair. On this day, as I approached my spot, I found a green lizard sunning himself precisely where I wanted to sit down. He looked at me; I looked at him. Warily, he moved slightly to the right and I to the left. I sat down and settled in. We coexisted peacefully for hours.

My reading project for this day was the memoir of Iris Origo, an Anglo-American who in 1924 married an Italian and settled on a farm in Tuscany, where she wrote about Byron, the Italian poet Leopardi, Saint Bernardino of Siena, Francesco Datini, and others.

In *Images and Shadows* (1970), Origo surveys her long life and reflects philosophically about "time in the past":

> Bernard Berenson once said in his old age that if he were a beggarman on a street corner, he would stretch out his hand to every passer-by, begging for "more time, more time!" I do not agree with him. I should like, of course—for I enjoy living—to have a few more years (provided all my faculties remained) in which to watch my grandchildren growing up, to see a little more of the world and of the overwhelming changes that are taking place in it and, above all, to see a little more clearly into myself. But the time I would really beg for, at any street corner, would be *time in*

the past, time in which to comfort, to complete and repair—time wasted before I knew how quickly it would slip by.

Most of us, however well we may know that remorse is fruitless, carry in our memories some heavy burdens, and perhaps at least one so poignant that we can hardly bear to look back on it: a weight of sadness and regret, a knowledge that we have failed even those who needed us most—especially those, since with other people one is not upon that plane at all. Nor is it of much consolation to realize that almost everyone, while life is actually going on, is constantly being distracted by irrelevancies. Just as, in travel, one may miss seeing the sunset because one cannot find the ticket office or is afraid of missing the train, so in even the closest human relationships a vast amount of time and of affection is drained away in minor misunderstandings, missed opportunities, and failures in consideration or understanding.

*P*erhaps like Berenson, John was making an unconscious cry for "more time, more time" when he chose to marry a much younger woman who would make him younger as well, at least in his mind.

The only occasion on which I heard John speak an untruth occurred when my college friends from the East Coast passed through Seattle en route to Alaska. Since I was already dating John on a regular basis then, I made it a point to introduce them. During dinner, one friend asked John, "How old are your children?"

"They're in their twenties," he replied, too quickly. The truth was that both of his children had by then already slipped well over the thirty mark.

This experience returned to me as I sat eying my Arno River neighbor, the green lizard. He was at peace. And so was I, except that I gasped slightly as I realized that something else had just happened. I had always idealized John, repressing this experience and others like it. But now I was admitting to the faintest critical reaction of something John had done. How much illusion had I needed to consummate my romance with this man? Had I idealized John and was that ideal slipping? Was he becoming human, as he had not been before? Was this humanization of John something else that I needed in order to heal?

After reading Iris Origo's memoirs, I decided to visit her home, Villa La Foce, south of Siena, near Chianciano Terme and Montepulciano. It is open by appointment each Wednesday from 1 p.m. to 5 p.m.

Villa La Foce sits majestically on a hill overlooking a sweeping valley called Val d'Orcia which lies in a part of Tuscany that some Italians call "the badlands," a vast, lonely, and rugged terrain. Yet it's also a part of Tuscany steeped in history. The Etruscans toiled there in the fifth century B.C. and were followed by the Romans, the Lombards, and Carolingians. In the Middle Ages the pilgrim's road to Rome, Via Francigena, cut through this desolate valley, bridging its isolation with all of Christian Europe. In the era of city-states, Florence and Siena feuded. Weakened by the Black Death, Siena eventually succumbed to Florence in the siege of 1554–55. For years thereafter this lonely part of Tuscany lay forgotten in time. During World War II it served as a hiding place for anti-Fascist partisans, fugitives, and escaping Allied prisoners of war. Over the years, shepherds have coveted this land for their sheep, and truffle hunters for wild fungus.

My main interest in going to La Foce was to see Iris Origo's gardens. I had begun to explore Italian landscaping—in Florence, the Boboli Gardens; at Lake Maggiore, Isola Bella; at Lake Como, the gardens of Villa del Balbianello; in Rome, Villa Borghese. Not only was Iris Origo a respected writer, but also a horticulturist who between 1927 and 1939 hired the British architect Cecil Pensent to create from Val d'Orcia's barren wilderness an elegant formal Renaissance garden at La Foce.

In *Images and Shadows*, Origo refers to the solace the garden brought her during the grieving over the death of her young son, Gianni, who died in 1933 at the age of eight of tubercular meningitis: "the greater part of the eight happy years of his childhood had been spent at La Foce, and every inch of the house and garden, every field and tree, seemed full of his presence."

Origo portrays her grounds to be "an allegory of life itself: one passes from the warm, sheltered house into the formal garden, with its fountain and flowers and intricate box hedges, then coasts the hillside under the pergola of vines. The view opens out on to fields, the flowers become rarer; one passes into the path through the woods. Here it is darker; the wind stirs in the branches. A few steps more, walking uphill in the shade, and one has reached the still chapel, with those four stone walls around it."

When I read these lines, I couldn't help remembering the comfort that our own far more modest garden in Seattle brought me during John's long decline. In the midst of dying, it was a place about living with its profusion of rhododendron, camellia bushes and dahlias. It was a place about continuity. Yes, things alter their form, but nothing really ends. What passed away in the fall, languishing in the compost heap all winter, advanced new life in the spring.

Once on Origo's property, I saw lawns, wildflower meadows, beds of indigenous cyclamens, and a wisteria-draped pergola. Cypress trees framed a grotto carved of local stone. The extinct volcano,

Monte Amiata, towered across the landscape. I could well imagine how during World War II the hills around Val d'Orcia provided cover to fleeing escapees. Not far from the main house lay the private family chapel with graveyard where Gianni was buried in 1933 and where Iris and her husband, Antonio, now rest as well. Iris Origo's tombstone contains a quotation by St. Catherine of Siena: *Chi più conosce più ama, più amando più gusta,* "The more you know, the more you love, and by loving more, the more you enjoy."

On the weekend following my visit to La Foce, two dozen students and I traveled to Assisi in Umbria to hike to Eremo delle Carceri, a forest hermitage where St. Francis, Italy's patron saint, prayed and communed with the animals. It was supposed to be a simple hike, about forty-five minutes.

"You shouldn't miss it," Father Pietro had told us.

Legend has it that while in prayer on this mountain, Saint Francis exuded such radiance that the villagers in the valley below thought there were forest fires burning on the hillside. When the villagers arrived and formed bucket brigades, they saw nothing more fiery than Saint Francis in spiritual ecstasy.

To reach the hermitage, we could take a taxi or hike. I decided to join the students on foot.

We set off through the outer walls of Assisi and then veered left onto a steep and rocky trail. We knew generally where we were to go. "Up there," Father Pietro had told us as he pointed vaguely in the direction of the mountain. "You can't miss it. Just follow the signs. Sister Elizabeth will meet you at the entrance of the hermitage and show you around," he said, as we were about to leave Piazza del

Comune for the mountain. "I'll arrange for our dinner tonight and then meet you at the hermitage in a couple of hours."

As an aside he added, "Italians are bird hunters. It's estimated that until recently they killed maybe up to 200 million songbirds a year. Bird life on and around Monte Subasio stopped pretty much until the early 1980s when the Umbrian government outlawed hunting on that mountain. Ah! But these laws are broken all the time. See how many birds you can spot as you climb the mountain."

The trail's gravelly floor made it hard to grip the ground. Yet the students seemed to glide up the mountain while I straggled behind, berating myself for not having taken the easy way out, the taxi.

We climbed. We stopped to rest. We had no maps. We made random right turns, random left turns. More than an hour passed.

Feeling frustrated, a few students decided to dash ahead to scout possible solutions. They disappeared. Then other students dashed ahead to look for the scouts. Pretty soon everyone was gone. I was alone. Our forty-five-minute trek had by now consumed nearly two hours.

Ridiculous! Me! Trying to be a kid. Act your age!

Just as I was about to retrace my steps back to Assisi, which I could see in the distant valley below, Heather, a student I had befriended in our modern Italian novel class, came down the mountain toward me saying, "Rose Marie, would you like a drink of water?"

"Yeees!"

"Did they find where we're supposed to go?" I asked as I gulped the water.

"No. They're completely lost."

"Where are they?"

"About a kilometer up ahead."

Heather and I plodded up the mountain in silence. Ten minutes passed. Twenty minutes passed.

Eventually, Heather broke the monotony. "Would you like a cookie for energy?"

"Yeees!" I said, feeling more and more frustrated.

We sat down again. We ate cookies and drank more water.

After I had caught my breath, I said, "Thanks for helping."

"I'd want someone to do the same for my mother," Heather quipped.

To her I probably seemed a "gutsy little trooper," but because of my age, someone had to keep an eye on me—tactfully, of course—to let me save face.

As we sat, we scanned the skyline for bird life. It was eerie. In this place where St. Francis celebrated animals, virtually no twittering.

After resting, Heather and I gathered up our backpacks and marched on.

Periodically we paused again, ate more cookies, and drank more water.

During one of our stops, when Heather must have suspected that I was near collapse, she said, "Rose Marie, I know CPR."

Eventually we linked up with the rest of the students, who were by then stretched out in an open field, weighing the options. Hours had elapsed. Several of us, including Heather, decided to abandon this misadventure and return to Assisi to visit the Basilica di San Francesco. The others chose to forge ahead. Eventually they reached the hermitage four hours behind schedule, where a frantic Sister Elizabeth awaited them. Before day's end they had hiked a total of about twenty miles, many of them in circles.

After returning to Assisi, we, the renegades, first stopped for hot chocolate. Then we explored the basilica, including the tomb of St. Francis, one of the holiest sites in Christendom.

Finally, near the train station we visited still another basilica. Santa Maria degli Angeli houses a sacred ancient chapel called Porziuncola where it is said angels appear. St. Francis asked to be taken there when he felt death upon him. Tradition holds that it has become so impregnated with centuries of faith and prayer that any object held against its walls or placed upon its altar becomes empowered with extraordinary healing energies.

I placed a dozen rosaries on the chapel's altar. I knew that in the coming years many of my friends, some of whom are open to such beliefs, would need them. And as I lay a rosary there for John, I took another step in releasing him to God's loving care and releasing a part of my grief that still nestled, swelling and shrinking, in my chest.

CHAPTER 19

Santo Cielo

"Vocatus atque non vocatus, Deus aderit."
("Invoked and not invoked, God will be present.")
—LATIN PROVERB

After having visited all the famous Florentine churches to study their art, one day I stumbled onto an English-language church in the heart of the city. Here I found a melting pot of Americans abroad. Expatriates with independent means. Art scholars in Florence for a semester's sabbatical. Writers. Scribblers. Hedonists. Business people just passing through. Flocks of college students. Tourists. Even romantic retirees who chose to live out their days in the home of the Renaissance.

The church maintained a lending library of English-language books. It organized holiday dinners, concerts, and lectures. Most of all, this church offered me an adult English-speaking community. Sometimes I just needed a break from my young student companions at the university.

My new adult acquaintances asked me, "Why are you here?" "Where do you work?" "Where is your husband?" "Where are your children?" I had to answer with a whole new frankness that often left me feeling naked.

Usually I'd say that I was a recent widow and that I had come to Italy to get my life back together. For Italian-speaking people, I had learned to say, "*Mio marito è morto.*" (My husband is dead.) Inevitably these emotional Italians would respond with, "*Mi dispiace molto.*" (I am so sorry.) Then someone would ask, "*Come è morto?*" (How did he die?) I would answer, "Alzheimer's," a concept I realized even the most provincial Italian grasped.

It was becoming easier to talk about the affliction to strangers. And I did not choke up. I was gaining distance.

But still, it wasn't enough. Some people I met questioned what I was doing alone in Italy. I wasn't the traditional dressed-in-black widow tending the fires at home. Just a year after John's death I was "trotting around the world on my own," enrolled in a university in a foreign country where I had few language skills and knew hardly a soul. Some thought that was odd—even suspicious. *Is she running away from something? Emotionally unstable? A fugitive?*

To those who believed that at midlife women should sit contentedly on the sidelines, I tried to explain: "John's death was a wake-up call. I'm not going to live forever. I needed to put fewer things on hold."

Once when I was running through my litany of apologies, a parishioner from Scotland touched my hand and said, "May God bless you." It was a reprieve. I no longer had to justify my life.

Each year about 10,000 Brits and 15,000 Yanks try the laborious process of becoming Anglo-Florentines, I read in a booklet at the church, when in reality, for most, it takes a dozen years to gain even a peripheral foothold.

When I studied these often natty "incomers," and briefly imag-

ined myself among them, I, a European by birth, realized that somewhere in my journey I had crossed an invisible line and become
solidly American.

It gave me so much pleasure to know that.

Sometimes we must leave a place to value it.

On the first anniversary of John's death, October 17, I arranged a
memorial service in his honor. I put on a dress. When Teresa saw
that I was honoring the day by dressing up (usually I wore jeans), she
changed into a pastel brown wool suit. It was ill-fitting, with a hem-
line too long. But her heart brimmed with love. She came with me
to pray in the palazzo's chapel for a soul she had never met.

After the service, she invited me to have lunch with her and
Salvatore. We could talk while she cooked.

"Lunch today," Teresa announced, "will be *crostini* with olive
paste, *panzanella*" (a salad made of dry bread, basil, tomato, parsley,
and garlic in olive oil), "and as a main course, *pappardelle alla lepre*
(broad noodles covered with hare sauce)."

The memory during the memorial service of John's long dying had
blunted my appetite, but only temporarily.

Teresa was a good cook, although her kitchen took a beating.
Things spilled. Food fell to the floor from where it was quickly
retrieved and thrown back into the pot. Pans rattled. Utensils
clanked.

"*Santo cielo!*" (Good heavens) was the mildest of the protests I
heard after each disaster.

But, never mind!

With a practiced hand Teresa reached for her wine, sipped, threw in a few more mysterious ingredients and within seconds her repast was back on track.

At the first hint of browning garlic, Salvatore, wearing his usual tool belt, materialized in the kitchen. With calloused workman's hands, but with a smile that showed a generous supply of gold-inlaid teeth, he reached for my hand and said a warm, *"Buon giorno."*

Salvatore washed his hands in the kitchen sink and then filled his wine glass.

"Alla nostra," (to our health) he toasted, then dissolved into an easychair saying, *"Ah, che buono!"* (Ah, that's good)

Relaxed by the wine, Teresa smiled at Salvatore flirtatiously and said, "It has been a good marriage, *eh* Salvatore?"

"Sì, as long as I've done what I was told," he twinkled wickedly. Salvatore had fought his battles. Now it was just easier to fall into line.

Only once did I see conflict between them. Late one afternoon, I returned home from class and decided to check for messages at the reception desk. As I approached, I heard raised voices. As I drew closer, I realized that it was Teresa who was shattering the quiet.

"Non mi ascolta mai . . . ." (He never listens to me!)

"Glielo ho detto venti volte . . . ." (I told him twenty times.)

When I stepped into the reception area, I saw Salvatore, Teresa, and Father Pietro in a huddle. Father Pietro looked glum.

The moment they saw me, all talking stopped, yet the room crackled with tension.

"Buona sera," I said in an upbeat voice hoping to break the silence.

"Buona sera, Rosa," was the somber reply.

Father Pietro whispered in English, "Domestic problems—every marriage has them . . . ."

After collecting my messages and initiating another round of cheerful *buona seras*, I retreated quickly into the stairwell only to hear again, *"Sono stufa—non ne posso più . . . "* (Sick and tired—).

"*Me ne vado da questa casa. . . .*" (I'm leaving this house!)

John and I rarely experienced discord. Perhaps during our comparatively brief time together, we didn't have a chance to build up a stockpile of indictments and resentments. Perhaps our marriage was incomplete. His illness plucked the teeth of any anger I might have felt. Teresa and Salvatore's marriage seemed fuller and, oddly, more complete.

By morning the thunderstorm in the *pensione* had passed. As I walked through the reception area on my way to class, Salvatore, disheveled as ever, stood attentively next to Teresa's reception desk, awaiting his wife's orders for the day.

CHAPTER 20

Roma: Paradiso

"At last, for the first time—I live! It beats everything: it leaves
Rome of your fancy—your education—no where. It makes Venice,
Florence—Oxford—London seem like little cities of pasteboard."
—HENRY JAMES,
Letters to William James, Rome, 1869

"**I**f you confuse the Pantheon (Rome) with the Parthenon
(Athens) on an exam or in a term paper, you'll get an automatic F in
this course," Professor Raffanelli announced as she lectured on
ancient Rome in art history class.

On this particular day Professor Raffanelli's topic was the Roman
passion for Greek art. It was so great that the Romans often import-
ed original Greek artworks and copied them.

"Roman architecture, however, is a creative accomplishment so
unique as to silence all doubts of its autonomy."

To illustrate, she showed us a slide of the Temple of Fortuna Virilis,
no longer a hybrid of Greek and Etruscan design, but now distinctly

Roman, with interiors that showcased both images of worship and trophies of war. The Temple of the Sibyl, whom the Romans consulted because she could prophesy the future, carries the distinctly Roman imprimatur: concrete construction. Apparently, building with concrete had been invented centuries before in the Near East, but the Romans expanded its use, making it a primary construction material.

With these points comfortably established, Professor Raffanelli then devoted the rest of the class to the Pantheon, her favorite piece of architecture in all the world; hence, the threat about an F if we didn't identify it.

I had seen the Pantheon before, but idly, not as a student. Several years before, my niece, Grazia, was studying art in Rome and helping to put on an exhibition. Her mother, my sister Anne, and I flew in to see it. One day we met Grazia for an espresso in the Piazza della Rotunda, the cobblestone square facing the Pantheon. In the shadows of this quintessential Roman building, we dallied over coffee, and only as an afterthought ventured into it. Hoping probably to teach her mother and me something about ancient architecture, Grazia explained about the portico, the coffering and the oculus, but my interest in such things then was superficial.

*S*obered by the thought that a brief mental lapse might result in an "automatic F," we in art history jumped at the opportunity, soon after Professor Raffanelli's lecture, to go to Rome on an introductory weekend tour with Father Martini who had studied at its Gregorian University years before and knew it like a native. The Pantheon was on his itinerary.

It was to be a two-day tour. Someone calculated that it was cheaper to buy round-trip train tickets to Rome for each of our tour days than to pay for hotel rooms. Our Florence rooms were already paid for. The train between the two cities took just over two hours and rolled peacefully through the Italian countryside. If all else failed, during these approximately four hours of daily train rides, we could study.

On the first day we were to meet Father Martini by the Obelisk in St. Peter's Square at 10:30 a.m. To optimize our time in Rome, several students and I took the 6:30 a.m. train from Florence, arriving at *Stazione Termini* just after 8:30 a.m. Once in Rome, we each had our own agendas until the 10:30 appointment with Father Martini.

With my moneybelt in place and a firm grip on my purse to keep it safe from prying little fingers, I took a taxi to the Spanish Steps, for me always a happy starting point in that city. American Express is nearby. So is McDonald's. Taxis are readily available, and Via Condotti, Rome's fashionable shopping street, is an easy stroll. Best of all, the Spanish steps loom grandly, punctuated with festive red azalea planters. To the right of the steps is the Keats-Shelley Memorial House, to the left the Babington Tea Room. The Antico Caffè Greco, once frequented by such artists as Keats, Shelley, Byron, Liszt, and Wagner, is a stone's throw away.

Relaxed by the morning light, I sat on the Spanish Steps, resting against an azalea planter and savoring the scene. The hordes of tourists had not yet arrived. By noon it would be hard to find a seat, at least in the shade.

I want to close my eyes to taste the moment but I have to watch for pickpockets.

I am deliberately modestly dressed. Wedding band. Timex watch. Comfortable walking shoes. Nothing anyone would want, at least not at first glance.

But I am a foreigner. Probably an American. Probably somewhere I have a credit card. A passport.

I am a good target.

Carabinieri are everywhere. What are they expecting? Tiananmen Square?

To breathe it all in . . . to realize where I am and what I have . . . a city twenty-seven centuries old . . . antiquity in its purest form . . .

With a start I looked at my watch. I had only an hour until I was to meet Father Martini.

Before hailing another taxi for my ride to the Vatican, I wanted a cappuccino to brace myself for what lay ahead with Father Martini, who at nearly seventy, has the stamina of a young man and was the world's greatest guide. He was a full professor of history, a Latin scholar, and published author. "And now," he said modestly, "all I do is baby-sit."

What I liked about his tours was the whole sweep of history that he grasped and then synthesized, offering us only its essence.

He mentioned his weight on occasion.

"He eats," a mutual acquaintance said presumptuously, "to dull the fact that he has not loved."

"But he has," I answered. "He has loved God."

*W*hen I reached St. Peter's Square, the Vatican shimmered in a golden haze, and Bernini's open-armed colonnade reached out as if to say "welcome." Father Martini was waiting at the Obelisk. Instinctively, I looked up to the window where in 1963 I had seen Pope John XXIII bless the crowds, and I paused to realize that I was standing on the site where Peter is said to have met his martyrdom.

Only about three dozen students had surfaced, but then our tour was optional. We could peel away at any time. Clearly, some students who had boarded the early morning train with me had decided on other activities.

The sun in St. Peter's Square had begun to heat up. Romans kept saying the warm winds from the Sahara were fueling another inferno. We wanted shade. At 10:45, after looking far and wide and not seeing another fellow student on the horizon, Father Martini said, *"Andiamo."* With that we marched toward the Holy Doors of the Basilica and into the refreshing coolness that comes with such structures.

To the right of the Holy Doors is Michelangelo's *Pietà*. It evoked memories.

As John lay dying I had a strange need to keep a picture of the *Pietà* nearby. It represented John and me—our struggle—John, emaciated, dying—and me, cradling him, wanting to ease his agony. When I looked closely at the sculpture, I thought about the universality of suffering. No one is spared. Everyone takes his turn, some more grievously than others. But I also felt that buried deep within the *Pietà* lay seeds of hope, especially in the reposeful expressions on the faces of Mary and Jesus which suggested to me that perhaps, indeed, someday burdens will be lifted and peace will prevail.

*A*fter the *Pietà* we saw *The Foot of St. Peter*, now worn thin by the caresses of endless pilgrims over the centuries, the Papal Altar, Bernini's Baroque canopy above St. Peter's tomb, the burial monuments of the popes, and so on.

While in the Basilica some students chose to climb the 537 steps that lead to the summit of St. Peter's dome. After deciding where to meet again later, the rest of us fought our way around Vatican walls through clogged traffic en route to other treasures.

"Jesus, Mary, and Joseph!" Father Martini fussed as he tried to clear a path through a crosswalk in which cars stood bumper to bumper.

"If only you had worn your Roman collar," I complained to Father Martini, "maybe people would show us more respect."

"Wouldn't mean a thing," replied Father Martini. "You just have to bully 'em—show 'em you're tougher than they are."

Indeed, when Father Martini forged ahead, surely on wings of angels, and sometimes actually straddling fenders, he always prevailed.

Some in our group asserted that Italian drivers are insane, pedestrians are invisible, crosswalks are bullrings, and red lights are Christmas decorations that people forgot to take down.

And so my mind, brimming with the sights, smells, and sounds of dying when I first arrived in Italy, was now filling up with arches and vaulting systems. Had I sat home and contemplated only my sorrow, I would be grieving still. But in the mind, as in physics, two things cannot occupy the same space at the same time.

By midafternoon of the second day, after the Colosseum, the Roman Forum, and more churches, fountains, and piazzas than we could count, we finally reached the Pantheon.

"The best preserved of all the ancient Roman buildings," Father Martini effused, as he guided us through the original bronze doors and under the coffered dome, Europe's biggest until Brunelleschi built the one in Florence more than a thousand years later.

We marveled at the skylight.

"The Pantheon shows how the Romans elaborated upon the form of the Greek temple to create a building of proportions even more perfect than the Greeks," Father Martini continued.

We reviewed these proportions in detail, and peered at each of the recesses and the tombs of eminent Italians who are buried there.

When Father Martini was certain that we could not possibly con-fuse the Pantheon with the Parthenon, he proposed a quick look at Bernini's *Elephant* sculpture near the Jesuit church of the Gesù, and then a coffee break before heading off to our respective evening plans—for most of us, a train ride back to Florence.

"Let's have an espresso at Piazza Navona," Father Martini sug-gested to Frazer, the math major, Michael, another Jesuit who had just joined us that day, and me, the only ones from our tour group still hanging around.

In a glow of afternoon light, we walked along twisting streets until we reached the famous Piazza Navona, long ago a field of huts and vineyards, today one of Rome's most opulent squares lined with elegant sidewalk cafés and restaurants. We chose to sit directly in front of Bernini's "Fountain of Four Rivers."

The sun continued to bear down on us as we settled into our seats. I sought out a niche under an umbrella.

I love the Italian gregariousness and their colorful theaters where much of it plays out: their piazzas, *bars*, markets, and even churches. Italians have less mental illness than other societies, because they have each other. Their families are still intact. Their society is not yet fractured. And they express their feelings—laughing, crying, ranting, raving. (Remember Signora Bertucci?)

*E*veryone ordered an espresso except me. I wanted a foamy cappuccino and a *panino* to fortify me for my train ride back to Florence. Our waiter directed me inside to an appetizing, refrigerated display of sandwiches—some dripping with finely chopped mushrooms and garlic, others with thickly sliced late summer tomatoes and garden herbs, still others with sautéed peppers and creamy goat cheese. When our orders came, and my companions saw my *panino*, they ordered their own.

We sat contentedly watching the afternoon shadows widen across the piazza.

CHAPTER 21

Fail-Safe Aphrodisiacs

"O hidden riches! O prolific good!
—DANTE, *The Divine Comedy*

My favorite time of day in Florence was late afternoon. Work was done. Classes were over. The sun was setting. And the town, still bathed in a golden light, began to beat with life.

After my afternoon cooking class, when I wanted to feel the town's energy, I often took the long way home along the Arno River and across the Ponte Vecchio with its overhanging workshops to Oltrarno, the left bank of the river.

I like autumn in Florence—no crowds—only the Florentines and we, the semipermanent dwellers.

Originally the shops on the Ponte Vecchio accommodated butchers, tanners, and blacksmiths, but because of their noise and stench, a sixteenth-century duke threw them out and decreed that the shops be renovated to accommodate goldsmiths. It is still the "jeweler's bridge" today.

Our cooking instructor in Florence, Giovanni Rossi, was keen that we expand our taste beyond the delicious fare served in restaurants. "Florentine artistry is not just sequestered in museums and churches," he lectured us. "It is in the marketplace, on the street, everywhere, today."

Giovanni wanted us to understand that Italy is not only remarkable as a bellwether of international style, but also of food, art, architecture, music, fashion, and jewelry crafting.

Early in his course, he encouraged us to have at least a cup of coffee in the Excelsior, Florence's grandest hotel. It's on a thirteenth-century square near the Arno and epitomizes Florentine luxury. He knew most in our class were on student budgets and that a modest beverage such as an espresso or a soda in the hotel bar was probably all we could afford in such a place. Still, he urged us to study the hotel's decor, china, linens, menu, and service. He wanted us to notice the other guests. How they dressed. How they carried themselves. "Experience the best. Take some portion of it for yourself," he liked to tell us.

In the same vein, he suggested that we observe the goldsmiths' shops on the Ponte Vecchio. "See how they work with precious metals. Study their inventive designs, their sense of detail, and their types of finishes."

Sometimes I would pretend that my trips across the Ponte Vecchio were "homework," when in reality I devoured the sheer beauty of these baubles and imagined how I might wear them.

In spite of the allure of this bridge, the only thing I ever bought from the jewelry *ateliers* was a small silver statue of a collie, because it reminded me of Champ, my beloved companion who left me just before John entered my life.

This little inanimate object in no way replaces the unconditional love Champ lavished on me. But it does evoke the most affectionate memories. And although memories are substitutes, they are at times welcome ones.

$\mathcal{A}$s I crossed the Ponte Vecchio, I stopped midway, at the bust of Cellini, the most famous of all the Florentine goldsmiths, and rested my arms on the ancient stone wall that separated the teeming pedestrian traffic from the gurgling water below. As I paused near Cellini's bust, hoarding the moment like gold, as John liked to do, a fellow bridge pedestrian suddenly interrupted my thoughts with, *"Scusi, Signora . . . per favore . . . photograph?"* He pointed to his camera and then his family.

"Sì, con piacere," I answered, happy to help.

The group lined up so that the setting sun from Ponte Santa Trinità highlighted their smiling faces.

Click!

"Grazie mille," the man said as he took back his camera.

"Prego," I responded as we parted and I resumed my trek across the Ponte Vecchio past still more jewelry stores. In one of them, I spotted a ring very much like the one John had given me upon our engagement—a small sapphire with two tiny diamonds on either side.

I remembered how John proposed.

We were sitting at his kitchen table before renovations. It wasn't any dropping-to-his-knees routine, just a casual "What kind of ring do you want?"

Since I wanted to bring a little more definition into our exchange, I asked, "Ring for what?"

"Our engagement, silly," he said with a laugh.

"Ohhhh," I said pretending surprise. "Sapphires and diamonds would be nice," I teased.

"Right-o," he said with a flourish. "That's what it'll be."

John liked goals. If you gave him a mission, he was on it like a dog with a bone. And he tended to be literal. The linear accountant's mind.

A few days later, while having dinner in a fish restaurant in Kirkland on Lake Washington, he handed me a box with my beautiful engagement ring.

"It's gorgeous," I cried delighting in the brilliant sheen of the blue stone. "It's so perfectly framed with the two little diamonds."

Anxious to please, he said, "If you don't like it, we can exchange it for something else."

"But I do like it. I love it!" I said, nearly breathless.

I had thought my ring was one of a kind, but this one in Florence was nearly like it. John had inscribed the ring with the words *con amore*. "Italian is the most romantic language in the world," he liked to tell me.

Once across the Ponte Vecchio, I entered the Left Bank of Florence called Oltrarno. There I soon passed a *bar* that belonged to my cooking instructor's family—mainly to his brother, Massimo, although Giovanni invested in it modestly at the outset and now proudly marketed its virtues.

"The *bar* in Italy is a national institution," Giovanni lectured exuberantly in class one day. "It's central to the Italian way of life. It's a place of community . . . where we meet our friends and enjoy liquid libations."

I stepped inside the dark, wood-paneled establishment. Coming from the bright afternoon sunlight on the Ponte Vecchio into this cavern nearly blinded me, but as my eyes adjusted I saw a rustic decor—gleaming copper and brass pots, a walnut-stained wooden wine cellar, the inevitable hissing espresso machine, a tray of *panini* with salami, a cluster of young people enjoying cool beverages, and a round table of old men playing *scopa* and sipping red wine.

Italian *bar* etiquette requires that you first approach the cash desk, give your order and pay. The owner hands you a receipt that you then take to the *bar* attendant, again stating your wishes. He gives you what you want and tears a corner of this receipt to indicate that you have been served.

To the man at the cash desk, whom I assumed to be Giovanni's brother, I said, "*Buon giorno.* I attend Giovanni Rossi's cooking school."

"Ah, Giovanni, he's a good brother," the man gushed in broken English. With people waiting in line behind me, Massimo had to move our conversation along. With a smile he asked, "How may I help you?"

"An espresso, please." I replied while handing him the money.

After three gulps of my too-bitter beverage and waving good-bye to Massimo, I meandered through the darkening lanes of Oltrarno, reflecting on Giovanni who was the Italian we had all come to Italy to meet. Warm. Jovial. And sensual. He had opulent black hair and strong white teeth. A bit rotund and flushed, maybe from too much red wine, he spoke passionately about all things.

"Life is art!" he reminded us often.

Early in the fall Giovanni took us to the Mercato Centrale to browse the produce stalls, examine for ourselves the fresh fruits and vegetables, cheeses, fish, poultry, and meat. He emphasized that Italian cooking is seasonal. "You buy it today and fix it today," he told us. He showed us how to harvest chestnuts and fungi in the hills above Florence. He lectured on all seventeen varieties of pasta and all twelve assortments of *pane*. He carried on about *bruschetta*, which he said is not so much to subdue appetites, but to stimulate taste-buds. He praised garlic's taste-enhancing qualities, but caught everyone off guard when he told us that garlic is commonly recommended as an aphrodisiac.

"It stimulates amorous performance," Giovanni announced buoyantly.

The silence was suddenly electric.

Frazer, ever the critic of young (he said "immature") foreign students in Florence, looked around the room with an amused smile.

"They're levitating," he whispered as he watched their rapt attention.

"Nature offers a remarkable number of substances that arouse sexual desire," Giovanni said, aware that he was transporting his audience. "Anise, for example, has been known to cure impotence. The simple egg can jump-start tired old men."

Giovanni went on to extol the merits of the eggplant, the raw oyster, certain game birds, and even the testicles of some animals. He then listed the most common testicles coveted for this purpose.

"Bulls, monkeys, goats, and lions have the most acclaim," he said, as he feigned a scholarly posture.

We saw his sly smile.

As the class laughed uproariously and begged for more, Giovanni teased demurely, "This is not a sex education class. There are books on this subject." But I was quite sure he was well informed!

Perhaps we were now more attentive to his praises of pesto and arborio rice. We rapped about basil, rosemary, capers, olive oil, balsamic vinegar, dried beans, pine nuts, sun-dried tomatoes, and juniper berries. We memorized whole epics on sheep's cheese, grains, wines, pork, and beef. Best of all, we learned how to take Tuscany's simple and natural ingredients and transform them into gastronomic symphonies. And with Giovanni's guidance, we got a handle on the fine art of leisurely lunches, followed by espressos (never cappuccinos, as I already knew, which are for breakfast only), in cafés such as Gilli's and Rivoire, and we learned more about the *passeggiata,* which he said was for purposes of digestion.

As a backdrop to his cooking classes, Giovanni played Rossini, Verdi, and Puccini tapes. He dropped nuggets about the *Quattrocento* and *Cinquecento.* And you would have thought he had personally known Cosimo dè Medici, the first important Medici patron of the arts. Giovanni collected Italian sayings and more than once told us, *Meglio un giorno da leone che cento da pecora.* "Better one day as a lion than a hundred years as a sheep." For us students that thought encapsulated the early, feisty spirit of Florence that had ushered in the Renaissance.

Giovanni did what he loved. He cooked. He ate. And judging from the seven children he had sired, he profited from his own aphrodisiacal cooking. Zorba the Italian. Whenever we spoke to him about leaving Italy, he always answered, *"Ritornerai, ne sono sicuro."* (You will return, I'm sure.) Then with a twinkle, he liked to add, *"Ci rivedremo."* (We will see each other again.)

I knew he meant it.

Since it was now early evening and I was hungry, I decided to go to my favorite *gran caffè* in Florence—the Rivoire on the Piazza della Signoria. Not for dinner. Just a snack. A large cup of hot chocolate overflowing with whipped cream. "Liquid chocolate," true aficionados called it.

As I crossed back over the Ponte Vecchio from Oltrarno, I dallied again in front of the jewelry shops that line this ancient bridge.

Suddenly, I felt a surge of freedom race through me—something I hadn't felt in years.

I can stand here all day if I want to, without feeling the pressure, the needs, of another human being.

John was impatient with me when I shopped. *Things* bored him. *Experience* excited him. I like both.

In that fleeting instant, I asked myself again, *Am I being disloyal to John's memory? Is it a betrayal to admit the slightest flaw in the ideal? Perhaps to view him more clearly is another step in the healing process, the very healing he would have wanted for me.*

It was almost dusk. With my new-found freedom, I strolled among the smartly dressed Florentine women in their natural fabrics—silks, wools, linens, and *puro cotone* (pure cotton—never synthetics). A sharp contrast to my student getups—jeans, sweatshirts, and windbreakers.

Fashion colors in Florence tend to be time-tested, never-go-wrong shades of black, navy, gray, camel, and ivory. And colors go according to season. A stylish Florentine woman told me: "Navy is worn only in the spring and summer, never in winter." The big fashion statement in winter is *visone* (mink). By November, Florentine women drip with it. And everything exudes quality. "Better fewer things, but good things," an Italian friend told me as she showed me her still intact, eight-year-old Max Mara coat.

Before my departure for Europe, a friend told me, "Don't even try to compete with Italian women." I'd always considered myself fairly well put together, but once I arrived in Florence I could see why my friend had said that.

For one thing, most Italian women are immaculately slim. Their diet is simple: coffee and maybe a piece of bread for breakfast. Pasta, vegetables, and possibly low-fat meat for lunch, the main meal, and a few simple cold cuts for dinner. *Basta!* (Enough!) They walk everywhere. They ride their bikes. Some roller-blade. Many smoke obsessively. And because of their slimness and innate good taste, they look great in whatever they wear.

A visitor can't miss the quiet self-assurance of Italian women. Their easy manner. Their ready laugh. But their confidence makes sense. They come from a society that adores and, therefore, nurtures its children. It's apparent everywhere. Fathers lovingly cuddle toddlers. Mothers proudly push baby carriages. Grandparents and other members of the extended family happily engage in child rearing.

*F*rom my seat outside the Caffè Rivoire, I glimpsed the Piazza della Signoria, historically the center of Florentine politics and now described by some tour guides as an "outdoor sculpture gallery." Indeed, from where I sat, I saw Michelangelo's *David.* It's a copy; the original *David,* now housed in the Galleria dell' Accademia, sat in this exact spot in the Piazza della Signoria until 1873, when the Florentine fathers decided that it needed to be protected from weather and pollution.

Just as I was eyeing Bandinelli's *Hercules and Cacus,* also in the Piazza, a graying Italian man in his late fifties passed by, about six feet two inches, immaculately dressed in a dark green overcoat with what looked like a long cashmere silk-lined scarf wrapped casually around his neck. He was walking briskly across the Piazza, conveying an aura of self-assurance—a man well loved—first by his *mamma,* then his wife and children. Probably a family's patriarch. He wore a wedding band and clearly knew where he was going—toward a jewelry shop just to the right of the *caffè* across a narrow pedestrian walk.

What's he shopping for? A birthday? An anniversary?

Once at the shop, he peered first into one side of the store window and then into the other, comparing and assessing as I watched him. Then he stepped inside. Through the store window I saw animated negotiations. He had found something and was bargaining. He laughed. He smiled. The shopkeeper offered him coffee. They gesticulated. A deal was cut. The man reached for his wallet, the shopkeeper for a box.

I imagined that his wife looked like a dream, like so many Florentine women—blond (maybe), brown eyed (probably), slim (certainly), and conservatively attired. I imagined that he was buying a gift for her. And after he gave it to her that evening, she would curl up in his arms . . . they would kiss . . .

Just then the shop's door opened. The man stepped out. He reached for his cell phone, holding it in his right hand, and with his thumb he deftly keyed in a number. His voice carried across the pedestrian walk.

"Angelina?" I heard him say radiantly, as he walked toward Via Calimala, behind the Caffè Rivoire.

"*Dolce, Signora?*" asked the waiter, startling me.

"*Sì, sì,*" I said absentmindedly and then gave my order for hot chocolate.

My daydream caught me off guard. I had been fantasizing about a relationship! After years of feeling nearly anesthetized about such things, I was physically attracted to another man.

Another unexpected step in the healing process.

*A*s I contemplated that brief interlude with mixed astonishment, guilt, and enjoyment (Giovanni's influence undoubtedly!), I noticed the couple next to me. New acquaintances from the university: American lawyer Norris Harting, and his wife, Barbara, from Seattle, were enjoying equally fine fare. Norris was in Florence to teach a three-week, pre-law intensive to our undergraduate students.

From the start Norris and Barbara struck me as fit. Norris might have been a wrestler when he was younger, Barbara definitely a jogger. He was solid and strong; she well oxygenated. Her skin glowed. Their children were grown and out of the house. They, too, were filling in some of the missing pieces of their lives. We had not had a chance to talk substantively, until now.

"We were sorry to hear about John," Norris offered right from the start.

"You knew him?" I said, amazed.

"Barbara and I play golf and John used to show up at some of the tournaments. This was a long time ago. We were real sorry to hear about his death."

"Thank you," I said. "It was an awful blow . . ." I was grateful that they had acknowledged John's passing.

To lighten the moment, Barbara then asked, "So, what brought you to Italy?"

I went through my usual explanation about how coming here was a chance to escape my recent past and "rehabilitate" myself.

Wanting to deflect the seriousness of our conversation, I asked, "And you?"

"Twenty years ago our daughter went through this Florence program. We came over to visit her and just fell in love with the place. Since then we've been back several times," Norris said.

After a second round of hot chocolate and too many cookies, we meandered back toward our respective homes—mine, Teresa's *pensione,* and the Hartings', a well-equipped faculty apartment just five minutes from the university.

In the soft evening light, we strolled along Via dei Calzaiuoli, making a left onto Via del Corso Borgo degli Albizi and on into our neighborhood.

The loneliness that enveloped me at the Bertuccis' when I first arrived in Italy has faded through Teresa's warmth and the university's inclusivity. Life is people and I need people.

With the exception of Andrew, Tony, and Paul, I had become more and more isolated during John's illness. And even those relationships were illness-centered. Not knowing what to say, and perhaps afraid they'd say the wrong thing, many of our friends had fallen away.

"I'd like to talk to you," Barbara said as we parted. Her frown told me she was upset about something. "May I call you?"

"Of course," I answered.

As I entered my *pensione*, I thought *It feels so good to have people in my life again. They are dissipating my grief.*

CHAPTER 22

A Road Map for Others

"As you go the way of life, you will see a great chasm.
Jump. It is not as wide as you think."
—NATIVE AMERICAN SAYING,
A Joseph Campbell Companion

As it turned out, my meeting with the Hartings was beneficial for my healing as well as for theirs.

The next day, Barbara approached me in the university library, where I was looking something up and she was reading the *International Herald Tribune*. Dressed in a long black Marina Rinaldi knit skirt with matching tunic, and black leather boots, she looked more Italian than many of the stylish Italian women parading around town. Barbara was an artist and her body was her canvas.

Dramatic brown hair. Bright red lips. Jangles of silver jewelry. But her face looked drawn, her eyes bloodshot, and she trembled.

"I didn't want to mention it with Norris there, but his older brother, Ron, sixty-nine, is in his third year of Alzheimer's disease," she said.

"Oh, Barbara, I'm so sorry," I replied.

"It's advancing fast, and the process is taking a terrible toll on Ron's wife, Jane, a woman I love with all my heart. We just received a fax from her today saying that she's going to place Ron in an institution."

Realizing that she wanted to talk, I asked her to step into the student lounge that adjoins the library. "The librarian is strict about not talking in here," I said. "I've already had a couple of run-ins with her over just whispering. If she catches me again, I'm dead."

Once settled in the lounge, where students chatted in small clusters as they awaited the day's mail from home, I said, "If he's already so impaired that Jane is considering placing him in an institution after just three years, then Ron clearly must have a fast-moving type of Alzheimer's. Usually people live with it for seven to ten years, although sometimes it kills within three years, and sometimes as long as fifteen years."

"Ron's on a torpedo," she said as she wiped her eyes. "He's at home right now, but Jane's losing control. Norris's dead-set against putting Ron away. He insists on finding a means of keeping him at home."

"Ron's his brother," I said, trying to offer perspective.

"Norris says you don't just unload a beloved family member into a hellhole, but Jane bears the brunt," Barbara countered angrily. After a pause, she added, "Norris really makes me mad. It's the usual chauvinistic dump-on-women thing. Jane's not that strong. She's the traditional wife and mother—the eternal nurturer who'll do anything for anybody. But that doesn't mean she's now got to take on Alzheimer's for God only knows how long."

"Can't she get help? Like from their kids?" I asked.

"Help from them?" she laughed shortly, smoothing her skirt that didn't need it with taut, shaking hands. "Their kids are into their own lives. They have jobs and kids of their own."

"What about home health aides?" I suggested.

"That costs money," Barbara lamented. "Jane and Ron have savings, but not enough to cover extended long-term care. How did you manage?" she asked.

"I barely did . . ." I answered.

Before I could go on, Barbara said, "I know you're busy, but could you have lunch with Norris and me? We're going home in a week, so it would have to be soon," Barbara added anxiously as she fidgeted with the newspaper. "Maybe there's something we can learn from your experience to share with Jane."

*T*wo days later Barbara, Norris, and I met at a nearby *ristorante,* well known for its white bean soup. We talked for hours, through lunch and into the afternoon.

When we first sat down, tensions between Norris and Barbara hung heavy. I didn't want to get into the middle of a fight. Having already told the Hartings about the *ristorante's* famous bean soup, I tried feebly to continue to soften the ice.

"Other Italians have nicknamed the Tuscans *mangiafagioli,* which means bean-eater. So many of their meals contain beans."

Barbara laughed nervously, suggesting that she wanted to be agreeable but was finding it hard.

"While looking through cookbooks in a bookstore the other day, I came across another old Tuscan saying—'The Florentine who eats beans licks the plates and tablecloths!'"

"Well, I hope we won't be reduced to that," Norris deadpanned under his breath. He pushed his glass of water around the table.

Barbara touched his hand as if to calm him. She knew he was chewed up about Ron. As if wanting to explain his ill humor, she whispered to me, "His bark is worse than his bite."

Norris caught her drift and halfheartedly steered the conversation back to the topic at hand, saying, "I guess Barb told you that Jane wants to put Ron away."

"It must be very hard on Jane," I replied.

"It's hard on Ron, too!" he retorted, clearly trying to keep his emotions in check. The bags under his eyes bulged. The sides of his mouth drooped. "What riles me," he continued, "is that he doesn't want to go, and Jane's ignoring his wishes. Even though he's failing, he still knows where he is and, dammit, I think he's got the right to be where he wants to. He's paid his dues."

The waiter brought our menus. After reviewing the possibilities, Norris ordered *bistecca alla fiorentina*, the signature meat dish in Italy, cooked over charcoal or wood ash and pulled from the flame while still rare; Barbara chose *trota alle erbe*, trout in herbs from one of Tuscany's many freshwater streams; and I opted for *trancia di tonno alla versigliese*, tuna flavored with rosemary, parsley, and garlic, baked in parchment.

After the waiter left, Barbara returned to our conversation, saying, "The family has some obligation toward Jane, too."

"Oh, I know." Norris said reluctantly. As an afterthought and with melancholy, he said, "It's just seems so unfair . . ."

"It always is," I replied. Then, still trying to ease the tension, I asked Norris, "What did Ron do before this happened?"

"You mean professionally?"

"Yes."

"He was an aerospace engineer, and I'm his kid brother. He was one hell of a big brother—a real mentor—got me out of more scrapes than I can count. And he worked like a dog all his life. Our parents always told us that hard work would be rewarded. Ron kind of held on to that dream. Delayed gratification. Now that he's supposedly free to enjoy life, he's lost his mind."

Norris was the first to reach for our Antinori, saying *"Salute,"* before drinking deeply. As he settled back into his chair, some of the angular lines in his face softened and his body language warmed. He looked at Barbara affectionately, realizing, probably, that he had been acting like a jerk. After another sip of red wine, he said, "I've had a better life than Ron. I guess I should say I've *made* a better life than Ron. The law has been good to me. I had the sense to take breaks. Every time my law firm allowed a sabbatical, I took it. Plus we've come over here often. But Ron just stayed home, except for a few budget trips to Hawaii, to save money for his kids' educations. He used to say, 'Just wait 'til I retire!' Now he barely recognizes us," Norris concluded between anger and grief.

"What're your thoughts on placing Alzheimer's patients in institutions?" Barbara asked me, as Norris listened warily.

"Well, that's obviously a family decision," I tried diplomatically. "In our case I knew of John's desperate wish to stay at home and I tried to make that happen. Sometimes you hear horror stories about facilities."

"Exactly," said Norris. "See?" he said, looking squarely at Barbara.

"But I must say I'm hearing better things about places these days," I pushed on. "As we live longer, Alzheimer's is becoming so common that society has to find better ways of dealing with it."

"That's for the future. Our problem is now," Norris cut in.

"If you keep Ron at home, Jane will need help. Either family members will have to pitch in or you'll have to hire home health aides, and that costs money. It took a lot of our savings to care for John at home. But I figured that it was his money. He earned it by sheer grit and he deserved a decent end."

"So does Ron," Norris countered.

"It might just come down to finances," Barbara reasoned.

"Talk with Ron's doctor," I suggested. "He'll have leads. Go check them out. Talk to families who have loved ones in the places he suggests."

Norris looked at Barbara with an expression of dread. Both sipped their wine in silence, Norris picking at the bread. Barbara poured olive oil into a side dish, sprinkling it generously with salt and pepper, then handed it to Norris for dipping.

A peace offering, I surmised. *Will he accept it?*

He paused, then took it. Tensions eased.

After a sigh, Barbara asked, "How can we help Jane?"

"Be available to her," I said.

"Of course," Norris said dismissively.

"It sounds simplistic," I argued, "but that's what helped me the most. Death's a scary thing. People shun it. They fear their own mortality, and if they're not thinking about that, then they're afraid they'll say the wrong thing. A lot of people dropped out of our lives when John first got sick—especially those on the periphery."

"You know, Jane's commented on that, how friends who used to come around don't anymore," Barbara said.

"The disease is just too overwhelming," I injected while Barbara enumerated those who didn't call anymore. "The Ericksens, the O'Briens, the Katzes . . ."

After the waiter had brought lunch to our table, and we had each taken first tastes, Barbara continued ruefully, "We've tried to be available to Jane and Ron. We've spelled Jane on weekends and sometimes in the evening when she's wanted to go to classes."

"Maybe we made a mistake in coming over here," Norris suggested gloomily. "Maybe we should've stayed home to help out."

I noticed that neither Barbara nor Norris had taken another bite, while I was relishing my fare. I noticed, too, that at a nearby table a young couple sat so in love, oblivious to the world, still so carefree, hardly eating, holding hands, maybe on their honeymoon. I couldn't discern their nationality, but it didn't matter. It was their blithe, unencumbered spirits that caught my attention.

We were like that once.

For a moment, I envied them.

"How's lunch?" I asked hoping to lift the Hartings' moods.

"Oh, fine," Barbara said politely. "Guess we're not real hungry after all." Then in a hushed tone she added, "We feel guilty enjoying ourselves while Jane and Ron struggle."

"Guilt's a big part of it," I assured her. "No matter what you do, you always feel you could have done more. Maybe you should focus on what you *can* do."

"That's easier said than done," Norris said sharply.

"What I know for sure is that we've got to find a way to help Jane take better care of herself," Barbara said.

"Respites are important. That's where *you* come in. Help her get breaks. "Also"—I brightened as I remembered—"get Jane to fix on something other than Ron and his inevitable decline."

"How do we do that?"

"Try asking her, 'What do you love?'" I proposed.

"I can tell you right now," Barbara replied adamantly, "that Jane's answer will be, 'Nothing, except Ron.' Jane's in too much pain right now to love anything outside her immediate situation."

"Probably her senses have shut down, just like mine did when John was dying," I said. "Well, then, consider asking her about what she *used* to love."

"Sports," Norris said immediately. "She and Ron were football nuts."

"Great! Going back to what we loved in the past can work, even though we don't feel like it in the present," I answered, borrowing heavily from what Dr. Reynolds had taught me. "Find a support group or, maybe even better, a counselor. It's true that some researchers suggest that not everyone needs counseling, because we are plenty resilient by ourselves. But a counselor helped me. Just make sure Jane knows that there are no set prescriptions or rules for mourning. I'll be happy to give you Dr. Reynolds's phone number."

"Thank you," Barbara said as she reached for a notepad in her purse. "I hope this isn't too upsetting for you to talk about. It's just that we want to know what we're in for, and no one will tell us anything."

"What's mine is yours," I joked dimly.

"It's been a year, hasn't it, since John passed away?" Barbara asked.

"Yes."

"I've heard that time doesn't heal, but experience does," Barbara offered. "Do you think it might be the *quality* of this experience here in Florence that's helping you with your healing process?"

"I think it is. Going back to school here has been incredibly helpful. To rekindle the past, first as a student, and then to be in a sensually charged place of long ago. To be hit with all this beauty, all these ideas, all these nice people. It's as if I've had a huge hole in my heart that has slowly begun to fill."

Just then the waiter suggested dessert.

"Heavens no!" Barbara said pointing to their still nearly full plates.

Wanting to express appreciation for his offer, Norris said, "*Grazie mille,*" in strained Italian. Then to Barbara and me, he proposed, "How about an espresso at Gilli's?"

"Good idea!" I said, welcoming the chocolate fix that I sometimes allow myself there.

It was an easy walk to Via de' Tornabuoni, along Via degli Strozzi to the Piazza della Repubblica where on this warm October day, we found Gilli's idling lazily in the afternoon sun.

We drank our coffees outside and watched the piazza swirl with life—a vendor roasted chestnuts, a flower woman sold mums, an old man sunned himself on a stone bench, and a young couple kissed.

A few weeks before I'd left for Italy, I'd had a long walk and talk in the Issaquah, Washington, Alps with my hiking companion, Sandra, a psychologist who specializes in lifespan development, particularly death and dying.

"But how will I know when I've worked through it?" I'd asked her, referring to a conversation I'd had with Dr. Reynolds about grief.

"No one can give you milepost signs, Rose Marie," she said to me. "But I think you're moving through it. Some people get stuck in grief, particularly because they get the label of 'widow' or 'widower,' and they almost feel as though that's a role they have to take on and live up to. Then, too, they may feel as though that's part of their identity and they'll lose a big part of themselves if they give it up. Losing a part of who you are is another death. But you're working it through, Rose Marie. I'm not worried about you."

Now I understood better what she had told me. I was no longer just a widow, but also someone who could help others along the way. In fact, eventually I might stop identifying myself as a widow altogether. It would always be a major part of who I am, because I would always love John, but perhaps no longer the first thing about myself that I revealed. Or even the most important. The most important was whatever I was growing into.

My conversation with the Hartings had launched me onto a new phase of my healing that I continue to this day—providing a road map for others to follow.

CHAPTER 23

Ladies in Red Dresses

"A man is not where he lives, but where he loves."
—LATIN PROVERB

$\mathcal{T}$eresa's *pensione* offered only a continental breakfast. For lunch and supper I had to eat out. Early in my stay in Florence, Father Pietro had recommended a nearby *trattoria* with about a dozen tables, where the owner's *mamma*, Benedetta Maccari, cooked the noon meal.

"It's a blue-collar place," Father Pietro said as if to apologize, "but it has good, solid Tuscan food." It became my mainstay eating establishment in Florence.

Indeed, when I sat at the appropriate table, I could watch the aproned and scarved Benedetta in the kitchen stirring her *zuppa di lenticchie*, adding vegetables, seafood, or meat to her risotto and working wonders with penne, spaghetti, gnocchi. When she made tripe it was gone by 12:30. And her sausages with beans and sage lasted at best until 12:45. I learned to come early, ideally before noon. If I had a favorite dish, it was *pollo in fricassea* (chicken in lemon sauce), which Benedetta lathered in garlic that had been browned in dark green, sedimented olive oil. Sometimes she added capers and lemon slices, and sometimes ripe olives.

*A*fter a while I felt like a familiar fixture there. Benedetta's son, Giuseppe, also owned a *bar/pasticceria* next door. I felt so comfortable with them that I could order a cappuccino after lunch instead of an espresso and I knew they wouldn't mind.

En route to Benedetta's each day, I passed, as early as midmorning, two or three plump, but stylishly clad (often in red) middle-aged women (in winter they wore mink). They stood at corners smoking, talking with one another and looking solicitous, especially toward men. One had blood-red hair, the other two had hair bleached too blond. Their faces were tired and they tried to hide their fatigue with heavy makeup. Sometimes they sat on chairs. Occasionally, a chair stood empty, but on it rested a carefully positioned lighter with cigarettes, suggesting "I'll be back soon."

This pattern was so consistent that one day I asked Father Pietro, "What about those fancy women en route to Benedetta's?"

"Oh, they're ladies of the night," he answered nonchalantly.

"But they're out there by day—in the morning, before noon?" I said.

"It's a red-light district," Father Pietro explained. "The neighborhood is full of artisans. These 'ladies' service them during their coffee and lunch breaks. They keep a running tab and bill their clients at the end of the month. The police look the other way."

"I have seen ladies of the night in other parts of Florence—near the American consulate, Cascine Park, and the train station in the late afternoon or in the evening," I commented. "They don't seem restricted to one place."

Father Pietro only shrugged as if to say that prostitution is a fact of life, that these are entrepreneurial women who had simply found a need and are filling it.

In Art History Professor Raffanelli had more to say about the ladies. Digressing from her lecture on Renaissance artists such as Leonardo da Vinci, Titian, and Raphael, she commented on an interesting although short-lived genre of the time: Italian salon courtesans in art.

"The courtesan of the Renaissance was far different from the common prostitute today," Professor Raffanelli said, her voice ringing through an attentive schoolroom. "For many she was a womanly ideal. In the eyes of some, a goddess."

At this comment, Heather frowned.

"These courtesans were often accomplished musicians, singers, and poets, not to mention highly skilled lovers," she continued. "Because of these talents, as well as their natural beauty and sensuality, they soon became companions to aristocrats, bankers, merchants, and clerics. In Venice, for example, courtesans were so celebrated that the state actually protected them, used them to attract business from abroad, and at times even to spy."

Professor Raffanelli then read from a book by Lynne Lawner titled
Lives of the Courtesans:

> The social forces that sparked the phenomenon of the courtesan con-
> verged at a particular time and place—in Rome at the papal court at the
> end of the fifteenth century. But why the "honest courtesan" came into
> being at exactly the time painters and writers "needed" her, and bankers,
> diplomats, and high-placed prelates were willing to pay for her, one can
> only guess.
>
> At the end of the fifteenth century, Rome was a city of celibates. The
> capital of Christianity, it was fast becoming the capital of prostitution. It
> would soon be a literary commonplace to remark that Rome itself had
> become one vast brothel. First of all, men greatly outnumbered women.
> Merchants and bankers jockeyed for important positions; courtiers seek-
> ing sinecures and Church benefits crowded around the papal court, and
> along with them came hordes of low ranking officials, clerks, and ser-
> vants in and out of the pay of important personages. All were bent on
> enjoying the perpetual *vita dulcedo* offered by Rome at that time. A real-
> istic if enormously cynical picture of this world emerges in Aretino's
> play *La cortigiana (The Courtesan,* 1525), in which the figure of the
> courtesan never appears, although Camilla of Pisa—a famous one—
> lurks offstage—both prey and predator in a society become a jungle of
> power and pleasure seekers.

To Lynne Lawner's words, Professor Raffanelli then added, "The
1490 census revealed 6,800 prostitutes in a population of less than
50,000."

My classmates sat wide-eyed. Then Heather raised her hand and
asked, "How did these courtesans work?"

"You want to know the business, *eh?*" teased the professor with a
smile.

"For future reference," Frazer suggested to the guffaws of the students and Heather's sheepish grin.

"Yes, Heather's interests are purely professional," said Molly, poking Heather in the ribs.

"Well, this is supposed to be a college-level course," said Professor Raffanelli. "I'd be remiss in my duties if I didn't respond."

After nearly two decades of teaching this course, Professor Raffanelli had a ready answer for Heather. She reached into her briefcase and pulled out a photocopied piece by Matteo Bandello, a short story writer from Lombardy who lived from 1485–1516, and read:

> There is a custom in Venice . . . namely that a courtesan takes six or seven lovers, assigning to each a certain night of the week when she dines and sleeps with him. During the day she is free to entertain whomever she wishes so that her mill never lies idle and does not rust from lack of the opportunity to grind grain. Once in a while, a wealthy foreigner insists on having one of her nights, warning her that otherwise she will not get a cent from him. In this case, it is her duty to request permission from the lover whose evening that would ordinarily be and to arrange to see him during the day instead. Each lover pays a monthly salary, and their agreement includes the provision that the courtesan is allowed to have foreigners as overnight guests.

Professor Raffanelli continued, "When the courtesan wasn't entertaining her clients, she cultivated herself to become ever more an object of desire. Many owned property, becoming early liberated women of independent means."

"What's the origin of the courtesan portraiture?" Molly asked.

"It goes back to the ancients who thought that when you paint a picture of a woman or write poetry about her, you own her."

With that Professor Raffanelli flashed slides on the wall: Raphael's *La Donna Velata*, sixteenth century, Palazzo Pitti, Florence; Titian's *Laura Dianti*, sixteenth century, Hans Kisters Collection, Kreuzlingen; and Giovanni Bellini, *Young Woman at her Toilet*, sixteenth century, Kunsthistorisches Museum, Vienna.

"Over the centuries few questions have puzzled art historians more than who sat for Leonardo da Vinci's *La Gioconda* (Mona Lisa)," Professor Raffanelli noted. "Some say the sitter was Lisa di Antonio Maria Gherardini, the wife of an important Florentine, Francesco del Giocondo, but others suggest that she might have been a courtesan."

"The influence of the Renaissance courtesan came to an end following the Council of Trent, in 1545, at which time more virtuous attitudes were adopted," Professor Rafanelli said as she folded up her lecture notes and dismissed the class for the day.

*A*s the months passed and I continued my almost daily trek to Benedetta's for lunch, the ladies of the night began to recognize me. We never spoke; we only nodded.

What set of circumstances brought these women to this—at this advanced age?

At the end of the semester when I told Giuseppi and Benedetta that I would soon be leaving for home, Benedetta sang out, "You come tomorrow at five for an espresso."

The next day not only did I find a steaming cappuccino, but Benedetta surprised me with some homemade *tiramisù*.

I asked Benedetta for her recipe. Here it is in translation:

1 POUND MASCARPONE CHEESE
4 EGG YOLKS, 2 EGG WHITES
2 TABLESPOONS COGNAC
3 OUNCES SUGAR
1/2 POUND LADY FINGERS
1 CUP STRONG COFFEE
GRATED CHOCOLATE

Beat egg yolks and sugar. Add mascarpone and cognac, mixing carefully. Beat egg whites until stiff and incorporate carefully into mixture. Set aside.

In serving dish: Quickly dip 1/2 of lady fingers in coffee and place on bottom of dish. Cover with 1/2 mascarpone mixture. Add another layer of coffee-dipped lady fingers. Top with rest of mixture. Cool in refrigerator two to three hours. Sprinkle with grated chocolate.

I made a copy of this recipe for the Hartings who were by now long home. Barbara had faxed me two or three times about how she and Norris had resumed their support of Ron and Jane in their battle with Alzheimer's. From experience, I knew the benefits of attending to small, daily pleasures, even, for some, those as simple as a new dessert recipe.

Arrivederci Firenze

"A change of heart is a strong motif of the Italian experience."
—SUSAN CAHILL, *Desiring Italy*

When my semester was nearly over and I prepared to go home, Teresa commented, "Rosa, you're different from the way you were when you came to us in September."

"I feel different," I told her. "I'm so happy, maybe the happiest I've ever been."

Teresa sat behind her reception desk working half-heartedly on her ledgers. It was midafternoon, *riposino* time and she wanted to talk.

"Espresso, Rosa?"

"*Sì, grazie,*" I answered knowing that this would be one of my last opportunities to visit with her.

With that, Teresa rose from her seat and wandered into the

kitchen, where the familiar clanking began. While she puttered, I studied the scene I had grown to know so well—the lobby/living room. On that day the well-scrubbed marble floor didn't smell like antiseptic; the ticking clock, usually punctual, ran late; the chintz curtains, often moving like graceful ballerinas, hung somberly; the wooden louvers, designed to shield Tuscany's unrelenting sun, today barricaded the cold.

It was now December and Teresa's *pensione* had a damp chill in the air. To assuage the cold, she wore a heavy sweater with a hand-knit wool shawl wrapped around her neck. When she returned with two espressos, she plunged into her favorite lobby easychair and reached to the side table for her knitting.

"What are you making now?" I asked.

"A sweater for Fabrizio," she answered as she held up a bundle of blue and green yarn that would eventually be a child's cozy jacket.

After sipping her espresso and getting a second wind, she picked up our conversation from several minutes before, saying, "And so you would recommend Florence to those recovering from a great loss such as yours?"

"Not necessarily. I didn't realize what I was doing when I decided to come here. I was just following a deep, unconscious calling, and I was lucky to pursue it with the American university."

As I drank my espresso and thought about her question, Teresa's knitting needles clicked quietly in predictable cadence.

"No single thing can heal us, I'm convinced of that," I continued. "It's a lot of ordinary little things that lift your heart and animate you and remind you of your innate worth and life's fundamental goodness."

"Ah, Rosa, you are good," Teresa said affectionately.

"I didn't always feel that way. Not when I was caring for John during his dying. I felt so inadequate, so helpless, like I was only good if I could reverse pain and suffering and even death."

After another swallow of my espresso, I added, "The things I've experienced here in Tuscany—companionship, storytelling, laughter, new ideas, incredible beauty, even good food and wine—they're available anywhere—on a float trip on the Colorado River or in a college program in California, or even at home, although for me, it was important to leave the scene of John's suffering—to put distance between that event and me—to replace memories of loss with bright new experiences."

Teresa listened empathetically until the phone rang. Then she hauled her tired body to the grating sound. If Teresa had asked me to say more about my new-found happiness, I would have quoted the wise person who said, "He who wishes to know great happiness must understand great sorrow."

But she didn't ask that. Instead, after completing her phone conversation, she said, "On Sunday, you, Padre Pietro and Padre Martini come to our house in the country for lunch. Alfonso, Francesca, Fabrizio, and my brother, Pippo, and his wife, Assunta, who look after our property, will be there."

"*Molte grazie,*" I said, honored to be drawn even closer into Teresa's warm circle.

On Sunday at the appointed hour and on the proper *binario* (track), Father Pietro, Father Martini, and I boarded the *locale* for Teresa and Salvatore's home on the rugged western coast south of Livorno overlooking the Tyrrhenian Sea.

Our train inched through cultivated countryside, stopping occasionally in well-preserved, honey-colored villages, accentuated with brown and gray, and bright roof tiles. Passengers tumbled off, others clambered on. It was *domenica*. The day of rest. The day to be with family. To worship God. To celebrate.

Our train moseyed past fortresses, watchtowers, and Roman villas. I saw terraced vineyards nestled strategically between foothills and valleys that optimized sunlight. Occasionally, belltowers and cypresses arched gracefully toward the sky. As I watched the Tuscan woodlands pass by, I remembered Teresa telling me that in this region hunting thrushes is almost a cult.

I hope we won't be served roast thrushes with chestnut-flour polenta, which Giovanni Rossi says is a Tuscan delicacy.

Teresa did say that for our *primo piatto* that day Assunta would prepare the province's renowned fish soup, *cacciucco*.

No thrushes in that dish, I know!

As our train plowed west, Father Martini napped, Father Pietro read, and I reflected on my life in this transforming land, with thoughts about my new friends.

Heather will leave Florence in April to finish her undergraduate degree in the United States. Frazer will balance his graduate work in mathematics with the start of an MBA next fall. Irish Fiona will visit me in Seattle next summer. Teresa, Gianni, Marcella, and Paolo consider Tuscany the center of the universe and won't budge from its borders. Giovanni Rossi brags that "Florence is the navel of the world." In a way he's right. A lot started here. As to the Bertuccis, after moving out, I went back to the signora's place once to pick up my mail. Our encounter was cordial.

When our train reached its destination, Salvatore awaited us with his ancient Fiat. After hearty rounds of *buon giorno*, Father Pietro and I piled into the back seat, leaving the front for Salvatore and Father Martini. Slowly, the Fiat tottered forward, groaning over hills, reeling into hollows, rebelling occasionally at steeper inclines, heaving, lurching, until finally it delivered us to an imposing rectangular vine-covered stone farmhouse with windows protected by heavy metal grating. Directly above the main entrance, a down comforter aired on a balcony under a dry but gray December sky. Silver-green olive trees framed the picture.

As we pulled into the drive, two German shepherd crossbreeds bounded to Salvatore's side of the car nearly knocking him over with exuberance.

"*Ciao belli!*"

"*Brava, Stella!*"

"*Buono, Raf!*"

"Our dogs were orphans and we adopted them several years ago," Salvatore explained. "Raf came first, then Stella. He was lonely, so we found him a companion. Pippo and Assunta care for them."

In the meantime, a familiar voice called, "*Benvenuta nella nostra casa!*" (Welcome to our house).

It was Teresa standing at the *portone*, the large main entrance. Fabrizio peeked from behind her skirt.

"Say *buon giorno*," Teresa whispered to Fabrizio who buried his face in her skirt determined to have none of this. His parents, Alfonso and Francesca, greeted us warmly as did Pippo and Assunta.

Teresa showed us to the living room filled with plump furniture and crystal knickknacks. A fire crackled. The dining room table, set for ten, glistened in the adjoining room. From the window, I saw lush blue-green fields and in the distance whitecaps on the Tyrrenian Sea. Stella and Raf lay peacefully on the floor near us listening with poised ears, reminiscent of Champ years before. Teresa offered us refreshments. We toasted each other. We chatted. In time, Assunta brought out Sunday lunch, the soup as Teresa had said, and for the main course *pollo affinocchiato allo spiedo* (fennel chicken cooked on a spit). Salvatore said grace. We ate. We laughed. Teresa put Fabrizio down for a nap. For dessert we enjoyed *torta della nonna* (grandma's tart) with espressos. After celebrating our community, and as the sun set, we climbed onto our *locale* for the train ride back to Florence and my last week.

*I*t was nearly Christmas and the two-week holiday break. Florence sparkled with festivity. Carousels. Concerts. Christmas shoppers. Hustle, bustle, but no tourists! In the piazzas vendors still roasted chestnuts, and flower women, now bundled against brisk autumn winds, still marketed their wares. Men dressed in loden coats, women in their minks. Children paraded in vibrant yellows, greens, and blues.

At daybreak on the Thursday following Teresa's luncheon in the country, as the taxi drove me to the Florence airport and my journey home to Seattle, I settled comfortably into the back seat, thinking, *Life is just in its infancy and mine to invent. Father Pietro's offer to find me a lover still stands. Someday I might take him up on it.*

Epilogue

Seven years have passed since John's death and six years since my healing pilgrimage to Tuscany.

In January 1996 I returned to Seattle to reestablish a home. I found a small house with a romantic interior courtyard that has as its focal point an Italian fountain that splashes happily all day long. My house is snug and lets me feel safe about leaving it from time to time. Twice since my return in 1996, I've gone back to Florence for summer school, and once to attend the university's Christmas tour to the Holy Lands. Each time it's as though I had never left. Fathers Martini and Pietro still work miracles with their flocks. Professor Rafannelli continues to raise the consciousness of her students. Teresa and Salvatore, I'm convinced, will die taking loving care of their assorted guests. Occasionally, I stay with them and she still calls me Rosa. Marcella and Paolo continue to run their hotels, but now in addition to managing their menagerie of dogs, they are the proud parents of twins. Whenever I visit Florence, I always look up our passionate and irrepressible cooking teacher, Giovanni.

"*Eh quanto tempo! Come sta?*" (A long time! How are you?) he says the moment he sees me.

"*Molte bene, grazie,*" I always answer.

Then we gossip about his work, food, wines, the family *bar*, and his children.

He always asks about my love life.

"It's important to love," he says with the air of a man who has loved much, "to offer yourself to life."

My niece, Grazia, the student of the Pantheon in Rome, eventually married a Roman and now lives just three minutes from the Vatican. In addition, she is the joyous mother of a little boy who at the age of not-quite-three already speaks two languages fluently: English from his mother, Italian from his father. Recently, he took a crayon and scribbled all over the newly painted living room wall, then stood back to admire his artwork and said proudly in English, "Nice!"

*O*ccasionally I'll be walking down a street in Seattle and suddenly I'll hear an exuberant "ROSE MARIE" being shouted in my direction.

I turn around and see before me a magnificent apparition, perfectly poised and elegant. Our eyes meet and inevitably the apparition will say, "Do you remember me?"

I pause, trying to connect the person so impeccably groomed before me with the undone look that we all cultivated so fastidiously in Florence. Suddenly, something in my brain will click in recognition and I'll cry "SUZIE!" (Sometimes it's "TAYLOR!" And still other times it is "JILL!")

We embrace, renewing a bond that will forever unite us: Italy, Florence, the university, the palazzo . . .

"What are you doing now? I always ask.

"I teach in Rhode Island," the apparition will say. Or "I'm a physician." "I'm a lawyer." Sometimes I hear "I'm a mother!"

Sometimes, I forget that most of my classmates in 1995 were then college juniors and about twenty-one years of age. In these succeeding years, they've had time to graduate from college, complete entire graduate programs, and in many cases to become fully developed human beings.

Their parents must be proud, I always think. I'm proud just because I got to know them.

My memory of John continues to loom large, although I remember less the afflicted soul he became, than the gallant spirit he was. When I think of him today, I think of Alfred, Lord Tennyson's beautiful poem, *Ulysses*:

> We are not now that strength which in old days
> Moved earth and heaven, that which we are, we are—
> One equal temper of heroic hearts,
> Made weak by time and fate, but strong in will
> To strive, to seek, to find, and not to yield.

I loved John's strength, his discipline, his love of life, and his determination to forge ahead against great odds.

What did I take away from my experience with him? More wonder and gratitude and a deeper bond with God.

As I wrote this book, I sometimes agonized about sharing so many personal details about his sad decline. I didn't have his permission to write this book. While he was well and even after he became sick, it never occurred to me to write about our struggle. It was only later— years later—that I began to think about letting his ordeal serve a larger purpose.

In the midst of our travail, I came across a book titled *In the Face of Death* by Peter Noll, a Swiss criminal lawyer, who upon being diagnosed with terminal cancer, decided to chronicle his impending death. At one point during his writing, he, too, questioned the appropriateness of laying out the grisly details. He wrote, "I have doubts whether all of these notes should really be published. Isn't this merely a critical discussion with myself, which concerns only me? No: death is universal, and what is universal ought to be public. This authorizes me to cross my threshold of shame, or shamelessness, if you prefer. I must demonstrate to others what is happening to me now and in the coming weeks. In the end, they will strip me naked anyway, before they wrap me in the winding sheets."

I'm comfortable now with my decision to reveal what I have revealed. John prized education. As the son of immigrant parents, he realized quickly how knowledge can empower a life. John believed in the family of man, the oneness that surrounds us, our interdependence and the responsibility each of us has to leave those among us better off than we find them. That means shedding light upon the shadowy path whenever we can.

Has anything changed for me since John's death and my restorative months in Tuscany? I try to live life more fully. I try to take less for granted. I try to garner fewer regrets. And I try to let love be my supreme value. I have my lapses, but at least I have my goals.

> "There is a land of the living and a land of the dead
> and the bridge is love,
> the only survival,
> the only meaning."
>
> —Thornton Wilder,
> *The Bridge of San Luis Rey*

Selected Bibliography

Abrams, M. H., ed. *The Norton Anthology of English Literature.* 2 Vols. New York: Norton, 1968.

Aeschylus. "The Eumenides," line 520. In *Quotations from Greek Authors,* translated by Craufurd Tait Ramage. Detroit, Mich.: Gale Research Company, 1968.

Albom, Mitch. *Tuesdays with Morrie.* New York: Doubleday, 1997.

Aristotle. "Nicomachean Ethics." In *The Ethics of Aristotle,* edited by John Burnet. Salem, N.H.: Ayer, 1988.

Barzini, Luigi. *The Italians.* New York: Simon and Schuster, 1996.

Bayley, John. *Elegy for Iris.* New York: St. Martin's Press, 1999.

Bloomfield, Harold H., et al. *How to Survive the Loss of a Love.* Allen Park, Mich.: Mary Books/Prelude Press, 2000.

Boone, J. Allen. *The Language of Silence.* New York: Harper and Row, 1970.

Boswell, James. *The Life of Samuel Johnson, LL.D.* New York: Heritage Press, 1963.

Byron, George Gordon. *The Poetical Works of Lord Byron.* New York: Oxford University Press, 1946.

Cahill, Susan, ed. *Desiring Italy.* New York: Ballantine, 1997.

Calvino, Italo. *Italian Folktales.* Orlando, Fla.: Harcourt, 1980.

Campbell, Joseph. *The Hero with a Thousand Faces.* Princeton, N.J.: Princeton University Press, 1968.

Dante. *The Divine Comedy*. Translated by Henry F. Cary for The Harvard Classics. New York: P. F. Collier, 1937.

De Angelis, Barbara. "An Invitation to God." In *For the Love of God*, edited by Benjamin Shield and Richard Carlson. Novato, Calif.: New World Library, 1997.

Dessaix, Robert. *Night Letters*. New York: St. Martin's, 1996.

Emerson, Ralph Waldo. "Love." In *Emerson's Essays*. New York: F. M. Lupton, 1894.

Estés, Clarissa Pinkola. *The Gift of Story*. New York: Ballantine, 1993.

Ferrucci, Piero. *What We May Be*. New York: Putnam, 1982.

Frankl, Viktor E. *Man's Search for Meaning*. New York: Pocket Books, 1984.

Frye, Northrop. *The Educated Imagination*. Bloomington: Indiana University Press, 1964.

Goethe, J. W. *Italian Journey*. Translated by W. H. Auden and Elizabeth Mayer. London: Collins, 1962.

Gunther, John. *Death Be Not Proud*. New York: Pyramid, 1971.

Guterson, David. *Snow Falling on Cedars*. New York: Vintage, 1995.

Harrison, Barbara Grizzuti. *Italian Days*. New York: Houghton Mifflin, 1989.

Hemingway, Ernest. *A Farewell to Arms*. New York: Scribner, 1929.

Hibbert, Christopher. *The House of Medici: Its Rise and Fall*. New York: William Morrow, 1974.

Houston, Jean. *The Possible Human*. Los Angeles: T. P. Tarcher, 1982.

Janson, H. W. *History of Art*. 5th ed. New York: Abrams, 1995.

Kabat-Zinn, Jon. "Falling Awake through Meditation." In *The Power of Meditation and Prayer*. Carlsbad, Calif.: Hay House, 1997.

Kushner, Harold S. *When Bad Things Happen to Good People*. New York: Avon, 1989.

Lawner, Lynne, *Lives of the Courtesans: Portraits of the Renaissance*. New York: Rizzoli, 1987.

Levey, Michael. *Florence: A Portrait*. Cambridge, Mass.: Harvard University Press, 1996.

Lewis, R. W. B. *The City of Florence: Historical Vistas and Personal Sightings*. New York: Henry Holt, 1995.

Liebman, Joshua L. *Peace of Mind*. New York: Carol, 1946.

Lindbergh, Anne Morrow. *Hour of Gold, Hour of Lead*. Orlando, Fla.: Harcourt, 1973.

Mace, Nancy L., and Peter V. Rabins. *The 36-Hour Day*. Baltimore: Johns Hopkins University Press, 1991.

Massie, Robert, and Susan Massie. *Journey*. New York: Knopf, 1973.

Mayes, Frances. *Under the Tuscan Sun*. San Francisco: Chronicle Books, 1996.

McCarthy, Mary. *The Stones of Florence*. Orlando, Fla.: Harcourt, 1963.

Moffat, Mary Jane, ed. *In the Midst of Winter*. New York: Vintage, 1992.

Montaigne. *The Complete Works of Montaigne*. Translated by Donald M. Frame. Stanford, Calif.: Stanford University Press, 1958.

Moore, Thomas. *Soul Mates*. New York: HarperCollins, 1994.

Nicholl, Donald. *Holiness*. New York: Seabury, 1981.

Noll, Peter. *In the Face of Death*. New York: Penguin Putnam, 1989.

Origo, Iris. *Images and Shadows*. London: John Murray, 1998.

———. *War in Val D'Orcia: An Italian War Diary: 1943–1944*. Boston: Godine, 1984.

Osbon, Diane K., ed. *A Joseph Campbell Companion*. New York: HarperCollins, 1991.

Peck, M. Scott. *The Road Less Traveled*. New York: Simon and Schuster, 1978.

Powers, Alice Leccese, ed. *Italy in Mind*. New York: Vintage, 1997.

Shain, Merle. *When Lovers Are Friends*. New York: Bantam, 1981.

Singh, Kathleen Dowling. *The Grace in Dying: How We Are Transformed Spiritually as We Die*. San Francisco: Harper-Collins, 1998.

Smith, Huston. *World's Religions*. New York: HarperCollins, 1994.

Stevenson, Burton, ed. *The Home Book of Proverbs, Maxims, and Familiar Phrases*. New York: Macmillan, 1948.

Stockdale, James B. *A Vietnam Experience: Ten Years of Reflection*. Stanford, Calif.: Hoover Press Publication, 1984.

Stone, Irving. *The Agony and the Ecstasy*. New York: Doubleday, 1961.

Tatelbaum, Judy. *The Courage to Grieve*. New York: Harper and Row, 1980.

Twain, Mark. *A Treasury of Mark Twain*. Edited by Edward Lewis and Robert Myers. Kansas City: Hallmark Cards, 1967.

Weinstock, Herbert. *Rossini: A Biography*. New York: Knopf, 1975.

Whitman, Walt. *Selected Poems*. New York: Random House, 1992.

Wilber, Ken. *Grace and Grit*. Boston, Shambhala Publications, 1991.

Wilder, Thornton. *Our Town: A Play in Three Acts*. New York: Perennial, 1998.

_____. *The Bridge of San Luis Rey*. New York: HarperCollins, 1955.

Wilton, Andrew, and Ilaria Bignamini, eds. *Grand Tour: The Lure of Italy in the Eighteenth Century*. London: Tate Gallery, 1996.

Vasari, Giorgio. *Lives of the Artists*. 2 Vols. London: Penguin, 1965.

Yapp, Peter, ed. *The Travellers' Dictionary of Quotation: Who Said What, about Where?* London: Routledge, 1983.